I0005180

Artificial Intelligence

Dr. R. Subha
Assistant Professor,
Department of Computer Science,
Karpagam Academy of Higher Education,
Coimbatore.

978-1-312-68239-9

First Edition: April – 2023

Lulu Publisher

ISBN: 978-1-312-68239-9

EDITORS PROFILE

 **Dr.R.Subha,** *M.Sc., graduate from Kodaikanal Christian College, Kodaikanal and M.Phil., graduate from Prist University, Tanjore. Her research work has been published in the National/International/ Journal s and in the conferences. Her research interests are in the area of Biometrics and Computer Networks. Dr.Subha perused her PhD from Mother Teresa Women's University, India, for her innovative research on Biometrics. She currently serves as the Assistant Professor in the department of Computer Science of Karpagam Academy of Higher Education, Coimbatore , India..*

Contents

Chapter I
Introducing AI

1.1 Introduction   1

1.2 Defining the Role of Data   9

1.3 Considering the Use of Algorithms   24

1.4 Pioneering Specialized Hardware   35

Chapter II
Considering the Uses of AI in Society

2.1 Seeing AI Uses in Computer Applications   42

2.2 Automating Common Processes   55

2.3 Using AI to Address Medical Needs   64

2.4 Relying on AI to Improve Human Interaction   76

Chapter III
Working with Software-Based AI Applications

3.1 Performing Data Analysis for AI   81

3.2 Employing Machine Learning in AI   88

3.3 Improving AI with Deep Learning   94

Chapter IV
Working with AI in Hardware Applications

4.1 Developing Robots   102

4.2 Flying with Drones   109

4.3 Utilizing the AI-Driven Car   119

Chapter V
Considering the Future of AI

5.1 Understanding the Nonstarter Application   132

5.2 Seeing AI in Space   142

5.3 Adding New Human Occupations   155

PREFACE

Artificial Intelligence starts by helping you understand AI, especially what AI needs to work and why it has failed in the past. You also discover the basis for some of the issues with AI today and how those issues might prove to be nearly impossible to solve in some cases. Of course, along with the issues, you also dis-cover the fixes for some problems and consider where scientists are taking AI in search of answers.

For a technology to survive, it must have a group of solid applications that actually work. It also must provide a payback to investors with the foresight to invest in the technology. In the past, AI failed to achieve critical success because it lacked some of these features. AI also suffered from being ahead of its time: True AI needed to wait for the current hardware to actually succeed. Today, you can find AI used in various computer applications and to automate processes. It's also relied on heavily in the medical field and to help improve human interaction. AI is also related to data analysis, machine learning, and deep learning.

AI has a truly bright future today because it has become an essential technology. This book also shows you the paths that AI is likely to follow in the future. The various trends discussed in this book are based on what people are actually trying to do now. The new technology hasn't succeeded yet, but because people are working on it, it does have a good chance of success at some point.

Authors

Chapter I

Introducing AI

1.1 Introduction

Artificial Intelligence (AI) has had several false starts and stops over the years, partly because people don't really understand what AI is all about, or even what it should accomplish. A major part of the problem is that movies, television shows, and books have all conspired to give false hopes as to what AI will accomplish. In addition, the human tendency to anthropomorphize (give human characteristics to) technology makes it seem as if AI must do more than it can hope to accomplish. So, the best way to start this book is to define what AI actually is, what it isn't, and how it connects to computers today.

Of course, the basis for what you expect from AI is a combination of how you define AI, the technology you have for implementing AI, and the goals you have for AI. Consequently, everyone sees AI differently. This book takes a middle-of-the-road approach by viewing AI from as many different perspectives as possible. It doesn't buy into the hype offered by proponents, nor does it indulge in the negativity espoused by detractors, so that you get the best possible view of AI as a tech-nology. As a result, you may find that you have somewhat different expectations than those you encounter in this book, which is fine, but it's essential to consider what the technology can actually do for you, rather than expect something it can't.

Defining the Term AI

Before you can use a term in any meaningful and useful way, you must have a definition for it. After all, if nobody agrees on a meaning, the term has none; it's just a collection of characters. Defining the idiom (a term whose meaning isn't clear from the meanings of its constituent elements) is especially important with technical terms that have received more than a little press coverage at various times and in various ways.

Saying that AI is an artificial intelligence doesn't really tell you anything meaningful, which is why there are so many discussions and disagreements over this term. Yes, you can argue that what occurs is artificial, not having come from a natural source. However, the intelligence part is, at best, ambiguous. Even if you don't necessarily agree with the definition of AI as it appears in the sections that follow, this book uses AI according to that definition, and knowing it will help you follow the rest of the text more easily.

Discerning intelligence

People define intelligence in many different ways. However, you can say that intelligence involves certain mental activities composed of the following activities:

»» Learning: Having the ability to obtain and process new information.

»» Reasoning: Being able to manipulate information in various ways.

»» Understanding: Considering the result of information manipulation.

»» Grasping truths: Determining the validity of the manipulated information.

»» Seeing relationships: Divining how validated data interacts with other data.

»» Considering meanings: Applying truths to particular situations in a manner consistent with their relationship.

»» Separating fact from belief: Determining whether the data is adequately supported by provable sources that can be demonstrated to be consistently valid.

The list could easily get quite long, but even this list is relatively prone to interpretation by anyone who accepts it as viable. As you can see from the list, how-ever, intelligence often follows a process that a computer system can mimic as part of a simulation:

- Set a goal based on needs or wants.
- Assess the value of any currently known information in support of the goal.
- Gather additional information that could support the goal.
- PART 1 Introducing AI
- Manipulate the data such that it achieves a form consistent with existing information.
- Define the relationships and truth values between existing and new information.
- Determine whether the goal is achieved.
- Modify the goal in light of the new data and its effect on the probability of success.
- Repeat Steps 2 through 7 as needed until the goal is achieved (found true) or the possibilities for achieving it are exhausted (found false).

Even though you can create algorithms and provide access to data in support of this process within a computer, a computer's capability to achieve intelligence is severely limited. For example, a computer is incapable of understanding anything because it relies on machine processes to manipulate data using pure math in a strictly mechanical fashion. Likewise, computers can't easily separate truth from mistruth (as described in Chapter 2). In fact, no computer can fully implement any of the mental activities described in the list that describes intelligence.

As part of deciding what intelligence actually involves, categorizing intelligence is also helpful. Humans don't use just one type of intelligence, but rather rely on multiple intelligences to perform tasks. Howard Gardner of Harvard has defined a number of these types of intelligence (see http://www.pz.harvard.edu/projects/ multiple-intelligences for details), and knowing them helps you to relate them to the kinds of tasks that a computer can simulate as intelligence (see Table 1-1 for a modified version of these intelligences with additional description).

Discovering four ways to define AI

As described in the previous section, the first concept that's important to under-stand is that AI doesn't really have anything to do with human intelligence. Yes, some AI is modelled to simulate human intelligence, but that's what it is: a simulation. When thinking about AI, notice an interplay between goal seeking, data processing used to achieve that goal, and data acquisition used to better under-stand the goal. AI relies on algorithms to achieve a result that may or may not have anything to do with human goals or methods of achieving those goals.

Understanding the History of AI

The previous sections of this chapter help you understand intelligence from the human perspective and see how modern computers are woefully inadequate for simulating such intelligence, much less actually becoming intelligent themselves.

However, the desire to create intelligent machines (or, in ancient times, idols) is as old as humans. The desire not to be alone in the universe, to have something with which to communicate without the inconsistencies of other humans, is a strong one. Of course, a single book can't contemplate all of human history, so the following sections provide a brief, pertinent overview of the history of modern AI attempts.

Starting with symbolic logic at Dartmouth

The earliest computers were just that: computing devices. They mimicked the human ability to manipulate symbols in order to perform basic math tasks, such as addition. Logical reasoning later added the capability to perform mathematical reasoning through comparisons (such as determining whether one value is greater than another value). However, humans still needed to define the algorithm used to perform the computation, provide the required data in the right format, and then interpret the result. During the summer of 1956, various scientists attended a workshop held on the Dartmouth College campus to do something more. They predicted that machines that could reason as effectively as humans would require, at most, a generation to come about. They were wrong. Only now have we realized machines that can perform mathematical and logical reasoning as effectively as a human (which means that computers must master at least six more intelligences before reaching anything even close to human intelligence).

The stated problem with the Dartmouth College and other endeavours of the time relates to hardware the processing capability to perform calculations quickly enough to create a simulation. However, that's not really the whole problem. Yes, hardware does figure in to the picture, but you can't simulate processes that you don't understand. Even so, the reason that AI is somewhat effective today is that the hardware has finally become powerful enough to support the required number of calculations.

Continuing with expert systems

Expert systems first appeared in the 1970s and again in the 1980s as an attempt to reduce the computational requirements posed by AI using the knowledge of experts. A number of expert system representations appeared, including rule based (which use if. . .then statements to base decisions on rules of thumb), frame based (which use databases organized into related hierarchies of generic information called frames), and logic based (which rely on set theory to establish relationships). The advent of expert systems is important because they present the first truly useful and successful implementations of AI.

A problem with expert systems is that they can be hard to create and maintain. Early users had to learn specialized programming languages such as List Processing (LisP) or Prolog. Some vendors saw an opportunity to put expert systems in the hands of less experienced or novice programmers by using products such as VP-Expert (see http://www.csis.ysu.edu/~john/824/vpxguide.html and https:// ww.amazon.com/exec/ obidos/ASIN/155622057X/ datacservip0f-20/), which rely on the rule-based approach. However, these products generally provided extremely limited functionality in using smallish knowledge bases.

In the 1990s, the phrase expert system began to disappear. The idea that expert systems were a failure did appear, but the reality is that expert systems were simply so successful that they became ingrained in the applications that they were designed to support. Using the example of a word processor, at one time you needed to buy a separate grammar checking application such as Right Writer (http://www. right-writer.com/). However, word processors now have grammar checkers built in because they proved so useful (if not always accurate) see https://www. washingtonpost.com/archive/opinions/1990/04/29/hello-mr-chips-pcs-learn-english/487 ce8a -18df- 4bb8-b53f-62840585e49d/ for details).

Overcoming the AI winters

The term AI winter refers to a period of reduced funding in the development of AI. In general, AI has followed a path on which proponents overstate what is possible, inducing people with no technology knowledge at all, but lots of money, to make investments. A period of criticism then follows when AI fails to meet expectations, and finally, the reduction in funding occurs. A number of these cycles have occurred over the years — all of them devastating to true progress.

AI is currently in a new hype phase because of machine learning, a technology that helps computers learn from data. Having a computer learn from data means not depending on a human programmer to set operations (tasks), but rather deriving them directly from examples that show how the computer should behave. It's like educating a baby by showing it how to behave through example. Machine learning has pitfalls because the computer can learn how to do things incorrectly through careless teaching.

Five tribes of scientists are working on machine learning algorithms, each one from a different point of view (see the "Avoiding AI Hype" section, later in this chapter, for details). At this time, the most successful solution is deep learning, which is a technology that strives to imitate the human brain. Deep learning is possible because of the availability of powerful computers, smarter algorithms, large datasets produced by the digitalization of our society, and huge investments from businesses such as Google, Facebook, Amazon, and others that take advantage of this AI renaissance for their own businesses.

People are saying that the AI winter is over because of deep learning, and that's true for now. However, when you look around at the ways in which people are viewing AI, you can easily figure out that another criticism phase will eventually occur unless proponents tone the rhetoric down. AI can do amazing things, but they're a mundane sort of amazing, as described in the next section.

Connecting AI to the Underlying Computer

To see AI at work, you need to have some sort of computing system, an application that contains the required software, and a knowledge base. The computing system could be anything with a chip inside; in fact, a smartphone does just as well as a desktop computer for some applications. Of course, if you're Amazon and you want to provide advice on a particular person's next buying decision, the smart-phone won't do — you need a really big computing system for that application.

The size of the computing system is directly proportional to the amount of work you expect the AI to perform.

The application can also vary in size, complexity, and even location. For example, if you're a business and want to analyse client data to determine how best to make a sales pitch, you might rely on a server-based application to perform the task. On the other hand, if you're a customer and want to find products on Amazon to go with your current purchase items, the application doesn't even reside on your computer; you access it through a web-based application located on Amazon's servers.

The knowledge base varies in location and size as well. The more complex the data, the more you can obtain from it, but the more you need to manipulate it as well. You get no free lunch when it comes to knowledge management. The -interplay between location and time is also important. A network connection affords you access to a large knowledge base online but costs you in time because of the latency of network connections. However, localized databases, while fast, tend to lack details in many cases.

1.2 Defining the Role of Data

There is nothing new about data. Every interesting application ever written for a computer has data associated with it. Data comes in many forms — some organized, some not. What has changed is the amount of data. Some people find it almost terrifying that we now have access to so much data that details nearly every aspect of most people's lives, sometimes to a level that even the person doesn't realize. In addition, the use of advanced hardware and improvements in algorithms make data the universal resource for AI today.

To work with data, you must first obtain it. Today, applications collect data manually, as done in the past, and also automatically, using new methods. However, it's not a matter of just one to two data collection techniques; collection methods take place on a continuum from fully manual to fully automatic.

Raw data doesn't usually work well for analysis purposes. This chapter also helps you understand the need for manipulating and shaping the data so that it meets specific requirements. You also discover the need to define the truth value of the data to ensure that analysis outcomes match the goals set for applications in the first place.

Interestingly, you also have data acquisition limits to deal with. No technology currently exists for grabbing thoughts from someone's mind through telepathic means. Of course, other limits exist, too — most of which you probably already know about but may not have considered.

Understanding Moore's implications

In 1965, Gordon Moore, cofounder of Intel and Fairchild Semiconductor, wrote in an article entitled "Cramming More Components onto Integrated Circuits" (http://ieeexplore.ieee.org/document/4785860/) that the number of components found in integrated circuits would double every year for the next decade. At that time, transistors dominated electronics. Being able to stuff more transistors into an Integrated Circuit (IC) meant being able to make electronic devices more capable and useful. This process is called integration and implies a strong process of electronics miniaturization (making the same circuit much smaller). Today's computers aren't all that much smaller than computers of a decade ago, yet they are decisively more powerful. The same goes for mobile phones. Even though they're the same size as their predecessors, they have become able to per-form more tasks.

What Moore stated in that article has actually been true for many years. The semiconductor industry calls it Moore's Law (see http://www.mooreslaw.org/ for details). Doubling did occur for the first ten years, as predicted. In 1975, Moore corrected his statement, forecasting a doubling every two years. Figure 2-1 shows the effects of this doubling. This rate of doubling is still valid, although now it's common opinion that it won't hold longer than the end of the present decade (up to about 2020). Starting in 2012, a mismatch began to occur between expected speed increases and what semiconductor companies can achieve with regard to miniaturization.

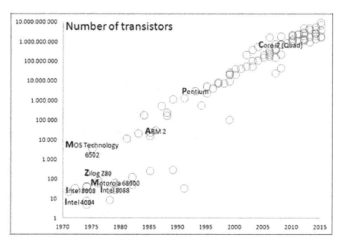

Physical barriers exist to integrating more circuits on an IC using the present silica components because you can make things only so small. However, innova-tion continues, as described at http://www.nature.com/news/the-chips-are-down-for-moores-law-1.19338. In the future, Moore's Law may not apply because industry will switch to a new technology (such as making components by using optical lasers instead of transistors; see the article at http://www. extremetech.com/extreme/187746-by-2020-you-could have- an- exascale speed-of-light-optical-computeron-your-desk for details about optical computing). What matters is that since 1965, the doubling of components every two years has ushered in great advancements in digital electronics that has had far-reaching consequences in the acquisition, storage, manipulation, and management of data.

Moore's Law has a direct effect on data. It begins with smarter devices. The smarter the devices, the more diffusion (as evidenced by electronics being everywhere today). The greater the diffusion, the lower the price becomes, creating an endless loop that drives the use of powerful computing machines and small sensors everywhere-. With large amounts of computer memory available and larger storage disks for data, the consequences are an expansion of data availability, such as web-sites, transaction records, measurements, digital images, and other sorts of data.

Using data everywhere

Scientists need more powerful computers than the average person because of their scientific experiments. They began dealing with impressive amounts of data years before anyone coined the term big data. At this point, the Internet didn't produce the vast sums of data that it does today. Remember that big data isn't a fad created by software and hardware vendors but has a basis in many scientific fields, such as astronomy (space missions), satellite (surveillance and monitoring), meteorology, physics (particle accelerators) and genomics (DNA sequences).

Although AI applications can specialize in a scientific field, such as IBM's Watson, which boasts an impressive medical diagnosis capability because it can learn information from millions of scientific papers on diseases and medicine, the actual AI application driver often has more mundane facets. Actual AI applications are mostly prized for being able to recognize objects, move along paths, or understand what people say and to them. Data contribution to the actual AI renaissance that molded it in such a fashion didn't arrive from the classical sources of scientific data.

The Internet now generates and distributes new data in large amounts. Our cur-rent daily data production is estimated to amount to about 2.5 quintillion (a number with 18 zeros) bytes, with the lion's share going to unstructured data like videos and audios. All this data is related to common human activities, feelings, experiences, and relations. Roaming through this data, an AI can easily learn how reasoning and acting more human-like works. Here are some examples of the more interesting data you can find:

»» Large repositories of faces and expressions from photos and videos posted on social media websites like Facebook, YouTube, and Google provide informa-tion about gender, age, feelings, and possibly sexual preferences, political orientations, or IQ (see https://www.theguardian.com/technology/2017/sep/12/artifi cial-intelligence- face-recognition-michal-kosinski).

»» Privately held medical information and biometric data from smart watches, which measure body data such as temperature and heart rate during both illness and good health.

»» Datasets of how people relate to each other and what drives their interest from sources such as social media and search engines. For instance, a study from Cambridge University's Psychometrics Centre claims that Facebook interactions contain a lot of data about intimate relationships (seehttps:// www.theguardian.com/ technology/2015/jan/13/ your-computer-knows-you-researchers-cambridgestanford-university).

»» Information on how we speak is recorded by mobile phones. For instance, OK Google, a function found on Android mobile phones, routinely records questions and sometimes even more: https://qz.com/526545/googles-been-quietly-recording-your-voice-heres-how-to-listen-to-and-delete-the-archive/.

Every day, users connect even more devices to the Internet that start storing new personal data. There are now personal assistants that sit in houses, such as -Amazon Echo and other integrated smart home devices that offer ways to regulate and facilitate the domestic environment. These are just the tip of the iceberg because many other common tools of everyday life are becoming interconnected (from the refrigerator to the toothbrush) and able to process, record, and transmit data. The Internet of Things (IoT) is becoming a reality. Experts estimate that by 2020, six times as many connected things will exist as there will be people, but research teams and think tanks are already revisiting those figures (http://www. gartner.com/newsroom/id/3165317).

Putting algorithms into action

The human race is now at an incredible intersection of unprecedented volumes of data, generated by increasingly smaller and powerful hardware. The data is also increasingly processed and analyzed by the same computers that the process helped spread and develop. This statement may seem obvious, but data has become so ubiquitous that its value no longer resides only in the information it contains (such as the case of data stored in a firm's database that allows its daily operations), but rather in its use as a means to create new values; such data is described as the "new oil." These new values mostly exist in how applications manicure, store, and retrieve data, and in how you actually use it by means of smart algorithms.

Algorithms and AI changed the data game. As mentioned in the previous chapter, AI algorithms have tried different approaches along the way, passing from simple algorithms to symbolic reasoning based on logic and then to expert systems. In recent years, they became neural networks and, in their most mature form, deep learning. As this methodological passage happened, data turned from being the information processed by predetermined algorithms to becoming what molded the algorithm into something useful for the task. Data turned from being just the raw material that fueled the solution to the artisan of the solution itself, as shown in Figure 2-2.

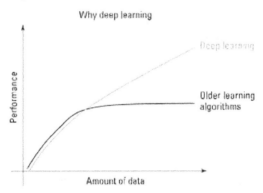

Thus, a photo of some of your kittens has become increasingly useful not simply just because of its affective value — depicting your cute little cats — but because it could become part of the learning process of an AI discovering more general concepts, such as what characteristics denote a cat, or understanding what defines cute.

On a larger scale, a company like Google feeds its algorithms from freely available data, such as the content of websites or the text found in publicly available texts and books. Google spider software crawls the web, jumping from website to web-site, retrieving web pages with their content of text and images. Even if Google gives back part of the data to users as search results, it extracts other kinds of information from the data using its AI algorithms, which learn from it how to achieve other objectives.

Algorithms that process words can help Google AI systems understand and anticipate your needs even when you are not expressing them in a set of keywords but in plain, unclear natural language, the language we speak every day (and yes, everyday language is often unclear). If you currently try to pose questions, not just chains of keywords, to the Google search engine, you'll notice that it tends to answer correctly. Since 2012, with the introduction of the Hummingbird update (http://searchengineland.com/google-hummingbird-172816), Google became better able to understand synonyms and concepts, something that goes beyond the initial data that it acquired, and this is the result of an AI process. An even more advanced algorithm exists in Google, named RankBrain, which learns directly from millions of queries every day and can answer ambiguous or unclear search queries, even expressed in slang or colloquial terms or simply ridden with errors. Rank-Brain doesn't service all the queries, but it learns from data how to better answer queries. It already handles 15 percent of the engine's queries, and in the future, this percentage could become 100 percent.

Using Data Successfully

Having plentiful data available isn't enough to create a successful AI. Presently, an AI algorithm can't extract information directly from raw data. Most algorithms rely on external collection and manipulation prior to analysis. When an algorithm collects useful information, it may not represent the right information. The following sections help you understand how to collect, manipulate, and automate data collection from an overview perspective.

Considering the data sources

The data you use comes from a number of sources. The most common data source is from information entered by humans at some point. Even when a system collects shopping-site data automatically, humans initially enter the information. A human clicks various items, adds them to a shopping cart, specifies characteristics (such as size) and quantity, and then checks out. Later, after the sale, the human gives the shopping experience, product, and delivery method a rating and makes comments. In short, every shopping experience becomes a data collection exercise as well.

Many data sources today rely on input gathered from human sources. Humans also provide manual input. You call or go into an office somewhere to make an appointment with a professional. A receptionist then gathers information from you that's needed for the appointment. This manually collected data eventually ends up in a dataset somewhere for analysis purposes.

Data is also collected from sensors, and these sensors can take almost any form. For example, many organizations base physical data collection, such as the number of people viewing an object in a window, on cellphone detection.

Facial recognition software could potentially detect repeat customers.

However, sensors can create datasets from almost anything. The weather service relies on datasets created by sensors that monitor environmental conditions such as rain, temperature, humidity, cloud cover, and so on. Robotic monitoring systems help correct small flaws in robotic operation by constantly analyzing data collected by monitoring sensors. A sensor, combined with a small AI application, could tell you when your dinner is cooked to perfection tonight. The sensor collects data, but the AI application uses rules to help define when the food is properly cooked.

Obtaining reliable data

The word reliable seems so easy to define, yet so hard to implement. Something is reliable when the results it produces are both expected and consistent. A reliable data source produces mundane data that contains no surprises; no one is shocked in the least by the outcome. Depending on your perspective, it could actually be a good thing that most people aren't yawning and then falling asleep when reviewing data. The surprises make the data worth analyzing and reviewing. Consequently, data has an aspect of duality. We want reliable, mundane, fully anticipated data that simply confirms what we already know, but the unexpected is what makes collecting the data useful in the first place.

Still, you don't want data that is so far out of the ordinary that it becomes almost frightening to review. Balance needs to be maintained when obtaining data. The data must fit within certain limits (as described in the "Manicuring the Data" section, later in this chapter). It must also meet specific criteria as to truth value (as described in the

"Considering the Five Mistruths in Data" section, later in this chapter). The data must also come at expected intervals, and all the fields of the incoming data record must be complete.

Making human input more reliable

Humans make mistakes — it's part of being human. In fact, expecting that humans won't make mistakes is unreasonable. Yet, many application designs assume that humans somehow won't make mistakes of any sort. The design expects that everyone will simply follow the rules. Unfortunately, the vast majority of users are guaranteed to not even read the rules because most humans are also lazy or too pressed for time when it comes to doing things that don't really help them directly.

Consider the entry of a state into a form. If you provide just a text field, some users might input the entire state name, such as Kansas. Of course, some users will make a typo or capitalization error and come up with Kansus or kANSAS. Setting these errors, people and organizations have various approaches to performing tasks. Someone in the publishing industry might use the Associated Press (AP) style guide and input Kan. Someone who is older and used to the Government Printing Office (GPO) guidelines might input Kans. instead. Other abbreviations are used as well. The U.S. Post Office (USPS) uses KS, but the U.S. Coast Guard uses KA. Meanwhile, the International Standards Organization (ISO) form goes with US-KS. Mind you, this is just a state entry, which is reasonably straightforward — or so you thought before reading this section. Clearly, because the state isn't going to change names anytime soon, you could simply provide a drop-down list box on the form for choosing the state in the required format, thereby eliminating differences in abbreviation use, typos, and capitalization errors in one fell swoop.

Manicuring the Data

Some people use the term manipulation when speaking about data, giving the impression that the data is somehow changed in an unscrupulous or devious manner. Perhaps a better term would be manicuring, which makes the data well shaped and lovely. No matter what term you use, however, raw data seldom meets the requirements for processing and analysis. To get something out of the data, you must manicure it to meet specific needs. The following sections discuss data manicuring needs.

Dealing with missing data

To answer a given question correctly, you must have all the facts. You can guess the answer to a question without all the facts, but then the answer is just as likely to be wrong as correct. Often, someone who makes a decision, essentially answering a question, without all the facts is said to jump to a conclusion. When analysing data, you have probably jumped to more conclusions than you think because of missing data. A data record, one entry in a dataset (which is all the data), consists of fields that contain facts used to answer a question. Each field contains a single kind of data that addresses a single fact. If that field is empty, you don't have the data you need to answer the question using that particular data record.

Considering data misalignments

Data might exist for each of the data records in a dataset, but it might not align with other data in other datasets you own.

For example, the numeric data in a field in one dataset might be a floating-point type (with decimal point), but an integer type in another dataset. Before you can combine the two datasets, the fields must contain the same type of data.

All sorts of other kinds of misalignment can occur. For example, date fields are notorious for being formatted in various ways. To compare dates, the data formats must be the same. However, dates are also insidious in their propensity for looking the same, but not being the same. For example, dates in one dataset might use Greenwich Mean Time (GMT) as a basis, while the dates in another dataset might use some other time zone. Before you can compare the times, you must align them to the same time zone. It can become even weirder when dates in one dataset come from a location that uses Daylight Saving Time (DST), but dates from another location don't.

Even when the data types and format are the same, other data misalignments can occur. For example, the fields in one dataset may not match the fields in the other dataset. In some cases, these differences are easy to correct. One dataset may treat first and last name as a single field, while another dataset might use separate fields for first and last name. The answer is to change all datasets to use a single field or to change them all to use separate fields for first and last name. Unfortunately, many misalignments in data content are harder to figure out. In fact, it's entirely possible that you might not be able to figure them out at all. However, before you give up, consider these potential solutions to the problem:

»» Calculate the missing data from other data that you can access.

»» Locate the missing data in another dataset.

»» Combine datasets to create a whole that provides consistent fields.

»» Collect additional data from various sources to fill in the missing data.

»» Redefine your question so that you no longer need the missing data.

Separating useful data from other data

Some organizations are of the opinion that they can never have too much data, but an excess of data becomes as much a problem as not enough. To solve problems efficiently, an AI requires just enough data. Defining the question that you want to answer concisely and clearly helps, as does using the correct algorithm (or algorithm ensemble). Of course, the major problems with having too much data are that finding the solution (after wading through all that extra data) takes longer, and sometimes you get confusing results because you can't see the forest for the trees.

Defining the Limits of Data Acquisition

It may seem as if everyone is acquiring your data without thought or reason, and you're right; they are. In fact, organizations collect, categorize, and store every-one's data — seemingly without goal or intent. According to Data Never Sleeps (https://www.domo.com/blog/data-never-sleeps-5/), the world is collecting data at the rate of 2.5 quintillion bytes per day. This daily data comes in all sorts of forms, as these examples attest:

»» Google conducts 3,607,080 searches.

»» Twitter users send 456,000 tweets.

»» YouTube users watch 4,146,600 videos.

»» Inboxes receive 103,447,529 spam emails.

»» The Weather Channel receives 18,055,555.56 weather requests.

»» GIPHY serves 694,444 GIFs.

Data acquisition has become a narcotic for organizations worldwide, and some think that the organization that collects the most somehow wins a prize. How-ever, data acquisition, in and of itself, accomplishes nothing. The book The Hitch-hiker's Guide to the Galaxy, by Douglas Adams (https://www.amazon.com/exec/ bidos/ASIN/ 1400052920/ datacservip0f-20/), illustrates this problem clearly. In this book, a race of super creatures builds an immense computer to calculate the meaning of "life, the universe, and everything." The answer of 42 doesn't really solve anything, so some of the creatures complain that the collection, categorization, and analysis of all the data used for the answer hasn't produced a usable result. The computer, a sentient one, no less, tells the people receiving the answer that the answer is indeed correct, but they need to know the question in order for the answer to make sense. Data acquisition can occur in unlimited amounts, but figuring out the right questions to ask can be daunting, if not impossible.

1.3 Considering the Use of Algorithms

Data is a game changer in AI. Recent advances in AI hint that for some problems, choosing the right amount of data is more important than the right algorithm. For instance, in 2001, two researchers from Microsoft, Banko and Brill, in their memorable paper "Scaling to Very Very Large Corpora for Natural Language Disambiguation" (http://www.aclweb.org/anthology/P01-1005) demonstrated that if you want a computer to create a model of a language, you don't need the smartest algorithm in town. After throwing more than one billion words within context at the problem, any algorithms will start performing incredibly well. This chapter helps you understand the relationship between algorithms and the data used to make them perform useful work.

However, no matter how much data you have, you still need an algorithm to make it useful. In addition, you must perform data analysis (a series of definable steps), to make data work correctly with the chosen algorithms. You don't get to take any shortcuts. Even though AI is intelligent automation, sometimes automation must take a back seat to analysis. Machines that learn by themselves are in the distant future. You won't find machines that know what's appropriate and can completely cut any human intervention today. The second half of this chapter helps you understand the role of expert systems, machine learning, deep learning, and applications such as AlphaGo in bringing future possibilities a little closer to reality.

Understanding the Role of Algorithms

People tend to recognize AI when a tool presents a novel approach and interacts with the user in a human-like way. Examples include digital assistants such as Siri, Alexa, and Cortana. However, certain other common tools, such as GPS routers and specialized planners (like those used to avoid automotive collisions, auto-pilot airplanes, and arrange production plans) don't even look like AI because they're too common and taken for granted as they act behind the scenes.

This is clearly the AI effect, as named and described by Pamela McCorduck, an America author who wrote a notable history of AI in 1979. The AI effect states that successful intelligent computer programs soon lose acknowledgment by people and become silent actors, while the attention shifts to AI problems that still require resolution. People become unaware of the importance of classic algorithms to AI and start fantasizing about AI created from esoteric technology or equating it to recent advances, such as machine learning and deep learning.

An algorithm is a procedure, which is a sequence of operations, usually dealt with by a computer that guarantees to find the correct solution to a problem in a finite time or tell you that no solution exists. Even though people have solved algorithms manually for literally thousands of years, doing so can consume huge amounts of time and require many numeric computations, depending on the complexity of the problem you want to solve. Algorithms are all about finding solutions, and the speedier and easier, the better. Algorithms have become hard-coded in the intelligence of humans who devised them, and any machine operating on algorithms cannot but reflect the intelligence embedded into such algorithmic procedures.

Understanding what algorithm means

An algorithm always presents a series of steps but doesn't necessarily perform all these steps to solve a problem. The scope of algorithms is incredibly large. Opera-tions may involve storing data, exploring it, and ordering or arranging it into data structures. You can find algorithms that solve problems in science, medicine, finance, industrial production and supply, and communication.

All algorithms are sequences of operations to find the correct solution to a problem in a reasonable time (or report back if no solution is found). AI algorithms distinguish themselves from generic algorithms by solving problems whose resolution is considered typically (or even exclusively) the product of human intelligent behaviour. AI algorithms tend to deal with complex problems, which are often part of the NP-complete class of problems (where NP is nondeterministic polynomial time) that humans routinely deal with by using a mix of rational approach and intuition. Here are just a few examples

»» Scheduling problems and allocating scarce resources.

»» Searching routes in complex physical or figurative spaces.

»» Recognizing patterns in image vision (versus something like image restoration or image processing) or sound perception.

»» Processing language (both text understanding and language translation).

»» Playing (and winning) competitive games.

Starting from planning and branching

Planning helps you determine the sequence of actions to perform to achieve a certain goal. It's a classic AI problem, and you find examples of planning in industrial production, resource allocation, and moving a robot inside a room. Starting from the present state, an AI determines all the possible actions from that state first. Technically, it expands the current state into a number of future states. Then it expands all the future states into their own future states, and so on. When you can't expand the states anymore and the AI stops the expansion, the AI has created a state space, which is composed of whatever could happen in the future. An AI can take advantage of a state space not just as a possible prediction (actually it predicts everything, though some future states are more likely than others) but also because AI can use that state space to explore decisions it can make to reach its goal in the best way. This is known as the state-space search.

Working with a state space requires use of both particular data structures and algorithms. The core data structures commonly used are trees and graphs. The favored algorithms used to efficiently explore graphs include breadth-first search or the deep-first search.

Building a tree works much like building a tree in the physical world. Each item you add to the tree is a node. Nodes connect to each other using links. The combi-nation of nodes and links forms a structure that looks like a tree, as shown in Figure 3-1.

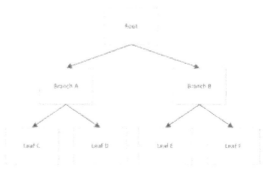

In looking at the tree, Branch B is the child of the Root node. That's because the Root node appears first in the list. Leaf E and Leaf F are both children of Branch B, making Branch B the parent of Leaf E and Leaf F. The relationship between nodes is important because discussions about trees often consider the child/parent relationship between nodes. Without these terms, discussions of trees could become quite confusing.

A graph is a sort of a tree extension. As with trees, you have nodes that connect to each other to create relationships. However, unlike binary trees, a graph node can have more than one or two connections. In fact, graph nodes often have a multitude of connections, and, most important, nodes can connect in any direction, not just from parent to child. To keep things simple, though, consider the graph shown in Figure 3-2.

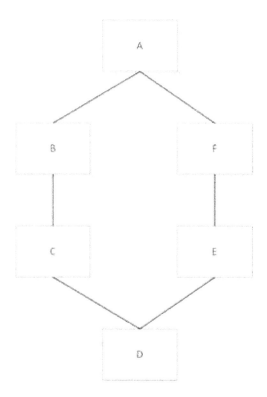

Graphs are structures that present a number of nodes (or vertexes) connected by a number of edges or arcs (depending on the representation). When you think about a graph, think about a structure like a map, where each location on the map is a node and the streets are the edges. This presentation differs from a tree, where each path ends up in a leaf node. Refer to Figure 3-2 to see a graph represented. Graphs are particularly useful when figuring out states that represent a sort of physical space. For instance, the GPS uses a graph to represent places and streets.

Graphs also add a few new twists that you might not have considered. For example, a graph can include the concept of directionality. Unlike a tree, which has parent/child relationships, a graph node can connect to any other node with a specific direction in mind. Think about streets in a city. Most streets are bidirectional, but some are one-way streets that allow movement in only one direction.

The presentation of a graph connection might not actually reflect the realities of the graph. A graph can designate a weight to a particular connection. The weight could define the distance between two points, define the time required to traverse the route, or provide other sorts of information.

Playing adversarial games

The interesting thing about state-space search is that it represents both AI's cur-rent functionality and future opportunities. This is the case of adversarial games (games in which one wins and the others lose) or of any similar situation in which players pursue an objective that conflict with the goals of others. A simple game like tic-tac-toe presents a perfect example of a space search game you may already have seen an AI play. In the 1983 film WarGames, the supercomputer WOPR (War Operation Plan Response) plays against itself at a blazing speed, yet it cannot win because the game is indeed simple and if you use a state-space search, you won't ever lose.

You have nine cells to fill with X's and O's for each player. The first one to place three marks in a row (horizontal, vertical, or diagonal) wins. When building a state-space tree for the tree, each level of the tree represents a game turn. The end nodes represent the final board state and determine a victory, draw, or defeat for the AI. Every terminal node has a higher score for winning, lower for drawing, and even lower or negative for losing. The AI propagates the scores to the upper nodes and branches using summation until reaching the starting node. The starting node represents the actual situation. Using a simple strategy enables you to traverse the tree: When it's AI's turn and you have to propagate the values of many nodes, you sum the maximum value (presumably because AI has to get the maxi-mum result from the game); when it's the adversary's turn, you sum the mini-mum value instead. In the end, you get a tree whose branches are qualified by scores. When it's the AI's turn, it chooses its move based on the branch whose value is the highest because it implies expanding nodes with the highest possibility to win. Figure 3-3 shows a visual example of this strategy.

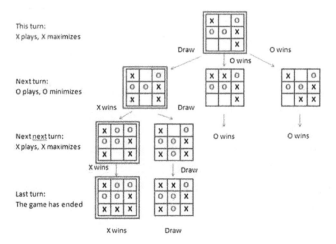

This approach is called the min-max approximation. Ronald Rivest, from the computer science laboratory at MIT, introduced it in 1987 (you can read his paper at https://people.csail.mit.edu/rivest/pubs/Riv87c.pdf). Since then, this algorithm and its variants have powered many competitive games, along with recent game-playing advances, such as AlphaGo from Google DeepMind, which uses an approach that echoes the min-max approximation (which is also found in the Wargames film of 1983).

Using local search and heuristics

A lot goes on behind the state-space search approach. In the end, no machine, no matter how powerful, can enumerate all the possibilities that spring from a situation. This section continues with games because they're predictable and have fixed rules, whereas many real-world situations are unpredictable and lack clear rules, making games an optimistic and favourable setting.

Checkers, a relatively simple game compared to chess or Go, has 500 billion billion (500,000,000,000,000,000,000) possible board positions, a number which, according to computations by the mathematicians at Hawaii University, equates to all the grains of sand on Earth. It's true that fewer moves are possible as a game of checkers progresses. Yet the number to potentially evaluate at each move is too high. It took 18 years using powerful computers (http://sciencenetlinks.com/ science-news/science-updates/checkers-solved/) to compute all 500 billion billion possible moves. Just imagine how long it could take on a consumer's computer to work out even a smaller subset of moves. To be manageable, it should be a very small subset of all the potential moves.

Optimization using local search and heuristics help by using constraints to limit the beginning number of possible evaluations (as in alpha pruning, where some computations are left out because they don't add anything to the search success). Local search is a general problem-solving approach that comprises a large range of algorithms that help you escape the exponential complexities of many NP problems. A local search starts from your present situation or an imperfect problem solution and moves away from it, a step at a time. A local search determines the viability of nearby solutions, potentially leading to a perfect solution, based on random choice or an astute heuristic (which means that no exact method is involved).

Discovering the Learning Machine

All the algorithmic examples so far are associated with AI because they're smart solutions that solve repetitive and well delimited, yet complex, problems requiring intelligence. They require an architect that studies the problem and chooses the right algorithm to solve it. Problem changes, mutations, or unusual characteristic displays can become a real problem for a successful execution of the algorithm.

This is because learning the problem and its solution occur once and for all at the time the algorithm appears in the software. For instance, you can safely program an AI to solve Sudoku (a popular game requiring you to place numbers in a board according to certain rules: https://www.learn-sudoku.com/what-is-sudoku. html). You can even provide flexibility that allows the algorithm to accept more rules or larger boards later. Peter Norvig, the director of research at Google, has written an extremely interesting essay on this topic (http://norvig.com/sudoku. html) that demonstrates how wise use of depth-first search, limiting the number of computations (otherwise the computations may take forever), using constraints, and exploring smaller branches first can make Sudoku solutions possible.

Unfortunately, not all problems can rely on a Sudoku-like solution. Real-life problems are never set in simple worlds of perfect information and well-defined action. Consider the problem of finding a fraudster cheating on insurance claims or the problem of diagnosing a medical disease:

»» A large set of rules and possibilities: The number of possible frauds is incredibly high; many diseases have similar symptoms.

»» Missing information: Fraudsters can conceal information; doctors often rely on incomplete information (examinations may be missing).

»» Problem rules aren't immutable: Fraudsters discover new ways to arrange swindles or frauds; new diseases arise or are discovered.

To solve such problems, you can't use a predetermined approach, but rather need a flexible approach and must accumulate useful knowledge to face any new challenge. In other words, you continue learning, as humans have to do throughout their lives to cope with a changing and challenging environment.

Introducing machine learning

Solutions capable of learning directly from data without any predigestion to render it as symbols arose a few decades before expert systems. Some were statistical in nature; others imitated nature in different ways; and still others tried to generate autonomously symbolic logic in the form of rules from raw information. All these solutions derived from different schools and appeared under different names that today comprise machine learning. Machine learning is part of the world of algorithms, although, contrary to the many algorithms discussed so far, it's not intended as a series of predefined steps apt to solve a problem. As a rule, machine learning deals with problems that humans don't know how to detail into steps, but that humans naturally solve. An example of such a problem is recognizing faces in images or certain words in a spoken discussion. Machine learning is mentioned in almost every chapter of this book, but Chapters 9 to 11 are devoted to disclosing how major machine learning algorithms work, especially deep learning, which is the technology powering the new wave of AI applications that reaches the news headlines almost every day.

Touching new heights

The role of machine learning in the new wave of AI algorithms is to in part replace, in part supplement, existing algorithms by rendering activities accessible that require intelligence from a human point of view that isn't easy to formalize as a precise sequence of steps. A clear example of this role is the mastery displayed by a Go-expert that, at a glance, understands threats and opportunities of a board configuration and grasps intuition of right moves. (Read the history of Go at http://www.usgo.org/brief-history-go.)

Go is an incredibly complex game for an AI. Chess has an average of 35 possible moves to evaluate in a board, and a game usually spans more than 80 moves, while a game of Go has about 140 moves to evaluate, and a game usually spans more than 240 moves. No computational power presently exists in the world to create a complete state-space for a game of Go. Google's DeepMind team in London developed AlphaGo, a program that has defeated a number of top-ranked Go players (see https://deepmind.com/research/alphago/). The program doesn't rely on an algorithmic approach based on searching an immense state-space, but instead uses the following:

»» A smart-search method based on random tests of a possible move. The AI applies a depth-first search multiple times to determine whether the first outcome found is a positive or negative one (an incomplete and partial state space).

»» A deep-learning algorithm processes an image of the board (at a glance) and derives both the best possible move in that situation (the algorithm is called the policy network) and an estimate of how likely the AI is to win the game using that move (the algorithm is called the value network).

»» A capability to learn by seeing past games by Go experts and by playing against itself, as did WOPR in the 1983 WarGames film. A recent version of the program, called AlphaGo Zero, can learn all by itself, without any human examples (see https://deepmind.com/blog/alphago-zero-learning-scratch/). This learning capability is called reinforcement learning.

1.4 Pioneering Specialized Hardware

You discover that one of the reasons for the failure of early AI efforts was a lack of suitable hardware. The hardware just couldn't perform tasks quickly enough for even mundane needs, much less something as complex as simulating human thought. This issue is described at some length in the move The Imitation Game (https://www.amazon.com /exec/obidos/ ASIN/B00RY86HSU/ datacservip0f-20/), in which Alan Turing finally cracked the Enigma code by cleverly looking for a particular phrase, "Heil Hitler," in each message. Without that particular flaw in the way that operators used the Enigma, the computer equipment that Turing used would never have worked fast enough to solve the problem (and the move had no small amount of griping about the matter). If any-thing, the historical account — what little of it is fully -declassified — shows that Turing's problems were more profound than the movie expressed (see https:// www.scienceabc.com/ innovation/ cracking-the-uncrackable-how-did-alan-turing-and-his-team-crack-the-enigma-code.html for details). Fortunately, standard, off-the-shelf hardware can overcome the speed issue for many problems today, which is where this chapter begins.

Relying on Standard Hardware

Most AI projects that you create will at least begin with standard hardware because modern off-the-shelf components actually provide significant processing power, especially when compared to components from the 1980s when AI first began to produce usable results. Consequently, even if you can't ultimately perform production level work by using standard hardware, you can get far enough along with your experimental and preproduction code to create a working model that will eventually process a full dataset.

Understanding the standard hardware

The architecture (structure) of the standard PC hasn't changed since John von Neumann first proposed it in 1946 (see the article at https://www.maa.org/ external_archive/ devlin/devlin_12_03.html for details). Reviewing the history at https://lennartb.home.xs4all.nl/coreboot/col2.html shows you that the processor connects to memory and peripheral devices through a bus in PC products as early as 1981 (and long before). All these systems use the Von Neumann architecture because this architecture provides significant benefits in modularity. Reading the history tells you that these devices allow upgrades to every component as individual decisions, allowing increases in capability. For example, within limits, you can increase the amount of memory or storage avail-able to any PC. You can also use advanced peripherals. However, all these elements connect through a bus.

Describing standard hardware deficiencies

The ability to create a modular system does have significant benefits, especially in business. The ability to remove and replace individual components keeps costs low while allowing incremental improvements in both speed and efficiency. How-ever, as with most things, there is no free lunch. The modularity provided by the Von Neumann architecture comes with some serious deficiencies:

»» Von Neumann bottleneck: Of all the deficiencies, the Von Neumann bottle-neck is the most serious when considering the requirements of disciplines such as AI, machine learning, and even data science. You can find this particular deficiency discussed in more detail in the "Considering the Von Neumann bottleneck" section, later in this chapter.

»» Single points of failure: Any loss of connectivity with the bus necessarily means that the computer fails immediately, rather than gracefully. Even in systems with multiple processors, the loss of a single process, which should simply produce a loss of capability, instead inflicts complete system failure. The same problem occurs with the loss of other system components: Instead of reducing functionality, the entire system fails. Given that AI often requires continuous system operation, the potential for serious consequences escalates with the manner in which an application relies on the hardware.

»» Single-mindedness: The Von Neumann bus can either retrieve an instruction or retrieve the data required to execute the instruction, but it can't do both. Consequently, when data retrieval requires several bus cycles, the processor remains idle, reducing its ability to perform instruction-intensive AI tasks even more.

»» Tasking: When the brain performs a task, a number of synapses fire at one time, allowing simultaneous execution of multiple operations. The original Von Neumann design allowed just one operation at a time, and only after the system retrieved both the required instruction and data. Computers today typically have multiple cores, which allow simultaneous execution of operations in each core. However, application code must specifically address this requirement, so the functionality often remains unused.

Considering the Von Neumann bottleneck

The Von Neumann bottleneck is a natural result of using a bus to transfer data between the processor, memory, long-term storage, and peripheral devices. No matter how fast the bus performs its task, overwhelming it that is, forming a bottleneck that reduces speed is always possible. Over time, processor speeds continue to increase while memory and other device improvements focus on density the capability to store more in less space. Consequently, the bottleneck becomes more of an issue with every improvement, causing the processor to spend a lot of time being idle.

Within reason, you can overcome some of the issues that surround the Von -Neumann bottleneck and produce small, but noticeable, increases in application speed. Here are the most common solutions:

»» Caching: When problems with obtaining data from memory fast enough with the Von Neumann Architecture became evident, hardware vendors quickly responded by adding localized memory that didn't require bus access. This memory appears external to the processor but as part of the processor package. High-speed cache is expensive, however, so cache sizes tend to be small.

»» Processor caching: Unfortunately, external caches still don't provide enough speed. Even using the fastest RAM available and cutting out the bus access completely doesn't meet the processing capacity needs of the processor. Consequently, vendors started adding internal memory — a cache smaller than the external cache, but with even faster access because it's part of the processor.

»» Prefetching: The problem with caches is that they prove useful only when they contain the correct data.

Unfortunately, cache hits prove low in applications that use a lot of data and perform a wide variety of tasks. The next step in making processors work faster is to guess which data the application will require next and load it into cache before the application requires it.

»» Using specialty RAM: You can get buried by RAM alphabet soup because there are more kinds of RAM than most people imagine. Each kind of RAM purports to solve at least part of the Von Neumann bottleneck problem, and they do work within limits. In most cases, the improvements revolve around the idea of getting data from memory and onto the bus faster. Two major (and many minor) factors affect speed: memory speed (how fast the memory moves data) and latency (how long it takes to locate a particular piece of data). You can read more about memory and the factors that affect it at http://www. computermemoryupgrade.net /types-of computer- memory-common-uses.html.

Chapter II

Considering the Uses of AI in Society

2.1 Seeing AI Uses in Computer Applications

You have likely used AI in some form in many of the computer applications you rely on for your work. For example, talking to your smartphone requires the use of a speech recognition AI. Likewise, an AI filters out all that junk

mail that could arrive in your Inbox. The first part of this chapter discusses AI application types, many of which will surprise you, and the fields that commonly rely on AI to perform a significant number of tasks. You also discover a source of limitations for creating AI-based applications, which helps you understand why sentient robots may not ever happen or not with the currently available technology, at least.

However, regardless of whether AI ever achieves sentience, the fact remains that AI does perform a significant number of useful tasks. The two essential ways in which AI currently contributes to human needs is through corrections and suggestions. You don't want to take the human view of these two terms. A correction isn't necessarily a response to a mistake. Likewise, a suggestion isn't necessarily a response to a query. For example, consider a driving-assisted car (one in which the AI assists rather than replaces the driver). As the car moves along, the AI can make small corrections that allow for driving and road conditions, pedestrians, and a wealth of other issues in advance of an actual mistake. The AI takes a proactive- approach to an issue that may or may not occur. Likewise, the AI can suggest a certain path to the human driving the car that may present the greatest likelihood of success, only to change the suggestion later based on new conditions. The second part of the chapter considers corrections and suggestions separately.

The third main part of the chapter discusses potential AI errors. An error occurs whenever the result is different from expected. The result may be successful, but it might remain unexpected. Of course, outright errors occur too; an AI may not provide a successful result. Perhaps the result even runs counter to the original goal (possibly causing damage). If you get the idea that AI applications provide gray, rather than black or white, results, you're well on the road to understanding how AI modifies typical computer applications, which do, in fact, provide either an absolutely correct or absolutely incorrect result.

Introducing Common Application Types

Just as the only thing that limits the kinds of procedural computer application types is the imagination of the programmer, AI applications could appear in any venue for just about any purpose, most of which no one has thought of yet. In fact, the flexibility that AI offers means that some AI applications may appear in places other than those for which the programmer originally defined them. In fact, someday AI software may well write its own next generation (see https://www. technologyreview.com/s/603381/ai-software-learns-to-make-ai-software/ for details). However, to obtain a better idea of just what makes AI useful in applications, it helps to view the most commonly applied uses for AI today (and the potential pitfalls associated with those uses), as described in the sections that follow.

Using AI in typical applications

You might find AI in places where it's hard to imagine using an AI. For example, your smart thermostat for controlling home temperature could contain an AI if the thermostat is complex enough (see https://www.popsci.com/gadgets/article/2011-12/artificially-intelligent-thermostats-learns adapt -automatically for details). The use of AI, even in these particularly special applications,- really does make sense when the AI is used for things that AI does best, such as tracking preferred temperatures over time to automatically create a temperature schedule. Here are some of the more typical uses for AI that you'll find in many places:

»» Artificial creativity.

»» Computer vision, virtual reality, and image processing.

»» Diagnosis (artificial intelligence)

»» Face recognition

»» Game artificial intelligence, computer game bot, game theory, and strategic planning

»» Handwriting recognition

»» Natural language processing, translation, and chatterbots

»» Nonlinear control and robotics

»» Optical character recognition

»» Speech recognition

Realizing AI's wide range of fields

Applications define specific kinds of uses for AI. You can also find AI used more generically in specific fields of expertise. The following list contains the fields where AI most commonly makes an appearance:

»» Artificial life

»» Automated reasoning

»» Automation

»» Biologically Inspired Computing

»» Concept mining

»» Data mining

»» Email spam filtering

»» Hybrid intelligent system

»» Intelligent agent and intelligent control

»» Knowledge representation

»» Litigation

»» Robotics: behaviour based robotics, cognition, cybernetics, developmental robotics (epigenetic), and evolutionary robotics.

»» Semantic web

Considering the Chinese Room argument

In 1980, John Searle write an article entitled "Minds, Brains, and Programs" that was published in Behavioral and Brain Sciences. The emphasis of this article is a ref-utation of the Turing test, in which a computer can fool a human into thinking that the computer is a human (rather than a computer) using a series of questions (see the article at https://www.abelard.org/turpap/turpap.php for details). The basic assumption is that functionalism, or the capability to simulate specific characteristics of the human mind, isn't the same as actually thinking.

The Chinese Room argument, as this thought experiment is called, relies on two tests. In the first test, someone creates an AI that can accept Chinese characters, use a set of rules to create a response from those characters, and then output the response using Chinese characters. The question is about a story — the AI must interpret the questions put to it such that the answer reflects actual story content and not just some random response. The AI is so good that no one outside the room can tell that an AI is performing the required tasks. The Chinese speakers are completely fooled into thinking that the AI really can read and understand Chinese.

In the second test, a human who doesn't speak Chinese is given three items that mimic what the computer does. The first is a script that contains a large number of Chinese characters, the second is a story in Chinese, and the third is a set of rules for correlating the first item to the second. Someone sends in a set of questions, written in Chinese, that the human makes sense of by using the set of rules to find the location in the story containing the answer based on an interpretation of the Chinese characters. The answer is the set of Chinese characters that correlate to the question based on the rules. The human gets so good at this task that no one can perceive the lack of understanding of the Chinese language.

The purpose of the two tests is to demonstrate that the capability to use formal rules to produce a result (syntax) is not the same as actually understanding what someone is doing (semantics). Searle postulated that syntax doesn't suffice for semantics, yet this is what some people who implement an AI are trying to say when it comes to creating various rule-based engines, such as the Script Applier Mechanism (SAM); see https://eric.ed.gov/?id=ED161024 for details.

The underlying issue pertains to having a strong AI, one that actually understands what it's trying to do, and a weak AI, one that is simply following the rules. All AI today is weak AI; it doesn't actually understand anything. What you see is clever programming that simulates thought by using rules (such as those implicit in algorithms). Of course, much controversy arises over the idea that no matter how complex machines become, they won't actually develop brains, which means that they'll never understand. The Searle assertion is that AI will remain weak. You can see a discussion of this topic at http://www.iep.utm.edu/chineser/.

The arguments and counterarguments are interesting to read because they pro-vide significant insights into what truly comes into play when creating an AI.

Seeing How AI Makes Applications Friendlier

There are a number of different ways in which to view the question of application friendliness addressed by AI. At its most basic level, an AI can provide anticipation of user input. For example, when the user has typed just a few letters of a particular word, the AI guesses the remaining characters. By providing this service, the AI accomplishes several goals:

»» The user becomes more efficient by typing fewer characters.

»» The application receives fewer errant entries as the result of typos.

»» The user and application both engage in a higher level of communication by prompting the user with correct or enhanced terms that the user might not otherwise remember, avoiding alternative terms that the computer may not recognize.

An AI can also learn from previous user input in reorganizing suggestions in a way that works with the user's method of performing tasks. This next level of interaction falls within the realm of suggestions described in the "Making Suggestions" section, later in this chapter. Suggestions can also include providing the user with ideas that the user might not have considered otherwise.

Performing Corrections Automatically

Humans constantly correct everything. It isn't a matter of everything being wrong. Rather, it's a matter of making everything slightly better (or at least trying to make it better). Even when humans manage to achieve just the right level of rightness at a particular moment, a new experience brings that level of rightness into question because now the person has additional data by which to judge the whole question of what constitutes right in a particular situation. To fully mimic human intelligence, AI must also have this capability to constantly correct the results it provides, even when such results would provide a positive result. The following sections discuss the issue of correctness and examine how automated corrections sometimes fail.

Considering the kinds of corrections

When most people think about AI and correction, they think about the spell checker or grammar checker. A person makes a mistake (or at least the AI thinks so) and the AI corrects this mistake so that the typed document is as accurate as possible. Of course, humans make lots of mistakes, so having an AI to correct them is a good idea.

Corrections can take all sorts of forms and not necessarily mean that an error has occurred or will occur in the future. For example, a car could assist a driver by making constant lane position corrections. The driver might be well within the limits of safe driving, but the AI could provide these micro corrections to help ensure that the driver remains safe.

Taking the whole correction scenario further, the car in front of the car containing the AI makes a sudden stop because of a deer in the road. The driver of the current car hasn't committed any sort of error. However, the AI can react faster than the driver can and acts to stop the car as quickly and as safely as possible to address the now-stopped car in front of it.

Seeing the benefits of automatic corrections

When an AI sees a need for a correction, it can either ask the human for permission to make the correction or make the change automatically. For example, when someone uses speech recognition to type a document and makes an error in gram-mar, the AI should ask permission before making a change because the human may have actually meant the word or the AI may have misunderstood what the human meant.

However, sometimes it's critical that the AI provide a robust enough decision-making process to perform corrections automatically. For example, when considering the braking scenario from the previous section, the AI doesn't have time to ask permission; it must apply the brake immediately or the human could die from the crash. Automatic corrections have a definite place when working with an AI, assuming that the need for a decision is critical and the AI is robust.

Understanding why automated corrections don't work

As related in the "Considering the Chinese Room argument" section, earlier in this chapter, an AI can't actually understand anything. Without understanding, it no capability to compensate for the unforeseen circumstance. In this case, the unforeseen circumstance relates to an unscripted event, one in which the AI can't accumulate additional data or rely on other mechanical means to solve. A human can solve the problem because a human understands the basis of the problem and usually enough of the surrounding events to define a pattern that can help form a solution. In addition, human innovation and creativity provides solutions where none are obvious through other means. Given that an AI currently lacks both innovation and creativity, the AI is at a disadvantage in solving specific problem domains.

To put this issue into perspective, consider the case of a spelling checker. A human types a perfectly legitimate word that doesn't appear in the dictionary used by the AI for making corrections. The AI often substitutes a word that looks close to the specified word, but is still incorrect. Even after the human checks the document, retypes the correct word, and then adds it to the dictionary, the AI is still apt to make a mistake. For example, the AI could treat the abbreviation CPU differently from cpu because the former is in uppercase and the latter appears in lowercase. A human would see that the two abbreviations are the same and that, in the second case, the abbreviation is correct but may need to appear in uppercase instead.

Making Suggestions

A suggestion is different from a command. Even though some humans seem to miss the point entirely, a suggestion is simply an idea put forth as a potential solution to a problem. Making a suggestion implies that other solutions could exist and that accepting a suggestion doesn't mean automatically implement-ing it. In fact, the suggestion is only an idea; it may not even work. Of course, in a perfect world, all suggestions would be good suggestions — at least possible -solutions to a correct output, which is seldom the case in the real world. The -following sections describe the nature of suggestions as they apply to an AI.

Getting suggestions based on past actions

The most common way that an AI uses to create a suggestion is by collecting past actions as events and then using those past actions as a dataset for making new suggestions. For example, someone purchases a Half-Baked Widget every month for three months. It makes sense to suggest buying another one at the beginning of the fourth month. In fact, a truly smart AI might make the suggestion at the right time of the month. For example, if the user makes the purchase between the third and the fifth day of the month for the first three months, it pays to start making the suggestion on the third day of the month and then move onto some-thing else after the fifth day.

Humans output an enormous number of clues while performing tasks. Unlike humans, an AI actually pays attention to every one of these clues and can record them in a consistent manner. The consistent collection of action data makes enables an AI to provide suggestions based on past actions with a high degree of accuracy in many cases.

Getting suggestions based on groups

Another common way to make suggestions relies on group membership. In this case, group membership need not be formal. A group could consist of a loose association of people who have some minor need or activity in common. For example, a lumberjack, a store owner, and a dietician could all buy mystery books. Even though they have nothing else in common, not even location, the fact that all three like mysteries makes them part of a group. An AI can easily spot patterns like this that might elude humans, so it can make good buying suggestions based on these rather loose group affiliations.

Groups can include ethereal connections that are temporary at best. For example, all the people who flew flight 1982 out of Houston on a certain day could form group. Again, no connection whatsoever exists between these people except that they appeared on a specific flight. However, by knowing this information, an AI could perform additional filtering to locate people within the flight who like mysteries. The point is that an AI can provide good suggestions based on group affiliation even when the group is difficult (if not impossible) to identify from a human perspective.

Obtaining the wrong suggestions

Anyone who has spent time shopping online knows that websites often provide suggestions based on various criteria, such as previous purchases. Unfortunately, these suggestions are often wrong because the underlying AI lacks understanding. When someone makes a once-in-a-lifetime purchase of a Super-Wide Widget, a human would likely know that the purchase is indeed once in a lifetime because it's extremely unlikely that anyone will need two. However, the AI doesn't under-stand this fact. So, unless a programmer specifically creates a rule specifying that Super-Wide Widgets are a once-in-a-lifetime purchase, the AI may choose to keep recommending the product because sales are understandably small. In fol-lowing a secondary rule about promoting products with slower sales, the AI behaves according to the characteristics that the developer provided for it, but the suggestions it makes are outright wrong.

Besides rule-based or logic errors in AIs, suggestions can become corrupted through data issues. For example, a GPS could make a suggestion based on the best possible data for a particular trip. However, road construction might make the suggested path untenable because the road is closed. Of course, many GPS applications do consider road construction, but they sometimes don't consider other issues, such as a sudden change in the speed limit or weather conditions that make a particular path treacherous. Humans can overcome lacks in data through innovation, such as by using the less travelled road or understanding the meaning of detour signs.

When an AI manages to get past the logic, rule, and data issues, it sometimes still makes bad suggestions because it doesn't understand the correlation between certain datasets in the same way a human does. For example, the AI may not know to suggest paint after a human purchases a combination of pipe and drywall when making a plumbing repair. The need to paint the drywall and the surrounding area after the repair is obvious to a human because a human has a sense of aesthetics that the AI lacks. The human makes a correlation between various products that isn't obvious to the AI.

Considering AI-based Errors

An outright error occurs when the result of a process, given specific inputs, isn't correct in any form. The answer doesn't provide a suitable response to a query. It isn't hard to find examples of AI-based errors. For example, a recent BBC News article describes how a single pixel difference in a picture fools a particular AI (see the article at http://www.bbc.com/news/technology-41845878). You can read more about the impact of adversarial attacks on AI at https://blog.openai.com/ adversarial-example-research/. The Kasperskey Lab Daily article at https:// www.kaspersky.com/blog/ai-fails/18318/ provides additional occurrences of situations in which an AI failed to provide the correct response. The point is that AI still has a high error rate in some circumstances, and the developers working with the AI are usually unsure why the errors even occur.

The sources of errors in AI are many. However, as noted in Chapter 1, AI can't even emulate all seven forms of human intelligence, so mistakes are not only possible but also unavoidable. Much of the material in Chapter 2 focuses on data and its impact on AI when the data is flawed in some way. In Chapter 3, you also find that even the algorithms that AI uses have limits. Chapter 4 points out that an AI -doesn't have access to the same number or types of human senses. As the TechCrunch article at https://techcrunch.com/2017/07/25/artificial-intelligence-is-not-as-smart-as-you-or-elon-musk-think/ points out, many of the seemingly impossible tasks that AI performs today are the result of using brute-force meth-ods rather than anything even close to actual thinking.

A major problem that's becoming more and more evident is that corporations often gloss over or even ignore problems with AI. The emphasis is on using an AI to reduce costs and improve productivity, which may not be attainable. The Bloomberg article at https://www.bloomberg.com /news/articles/2017-06-13/the-limits-of-artificial intelligence discusses this issue in some detail. One of the more interesting recent examples of a corporate entity going too far with an AI is Microsoft's Tay (see the article at https://www.geekwire.com/2016/ microsoft-chatbot-tay-mit-technology-fails/), which was trained to pro-vide racist, sexist, and pornographic remarks in front of a large crowd during a presentation.

2.2 Automating Common Processes

One of the longest uses of AI in a process is industrial utilization. Consider all the robots that now power the factories across the world. Even though AI-powered automation replaces humans, it also keeps humans safer by performing tasks generally considered dangerous. Oddly enough, one of the most significant issues for industrial accidents and a wealth of other issues is boredom (see https://thepsychologist.bps.org.uk/volume-20/edition-2/ boredom -work for details). Robots can perform those repetitive jobs consistently and without getting bored.

Developing Solutions for Boredom

Polls often show what people think they want, rather than what they do want, but they're still useful. When polled to see what kind of life recent college graduates wanted, not one of them said boredom (see https://www.huffingtonpost.com/ paul raushenbush/what-kind-of-life-do-you_b_595594.html). In fact, you could possibly poll just about any group and not come up with a single boring response. Most humans (saying all would likely result in an avalanche of email with examples) don't want to be bored. In some cases, AI can work with humans to make life more interesting — for the human, at least. The following sections discuss solutions for human boredom that AI can provide (and a few that it can't).

Making tasks more interesting

Any occupation, be it personal or for an organization, has certain characteristics that attract people and makes them want to participate in it. Obviously, some occupations, such as taking care of your own children, pay nothing, but the satis-faction of doing so can be incredibly high. Likewise, working as a bookkeeper may pay quite well but not offer much in the way of job satisfaction. Various polls (such as the one at http://www.careercast.com/jobs-rated/jobs-rated-report-2016-ranking-200-jobs) and articles (such as the one at http://www.nytimes. com/2010/09/12/ jobs/12search. html) talk about the balance of money and -satisfaction, but reading them often proves confusing because the basis for mak-ing a determination is ambiguous. However, most of these sources agree that after a human makes a certain amount of money, satisfaction becomes the key to main-taining interest in the occupation (no matter what that occupation might be). Of course, figuring out what comprises job satisfaction is nearly impossible, but interest remains high on the list. An interesting occupation will always have higher satisfaction potential.

Helping humans work more efficiently

Most humans, at least the forward-thinking ones, have some ideas of how they'd like an AI to make their lives better by eliminating tasks that they don't want to do. A recent poll shows some of the more interesting ways that AI can do this: https://blog.devolutions.net/2017/10/october-poll-results-which-tasks-in-your-job-would-you-like-to-be-automated-by-ai.html. Many of them are mundane, but notice the ones like detecting when a spouse is unhappy and sending flowers. It probably won't work, but it's an interesting idea nonetheless.

The point is that humans will likely provide the most interesting ideas on how to create an AI that specifically addresses that person's needs. In most cases, serious ideas will work well for other users, too. For example, automating trouble tickets is something that could work in a number of different industries. If someone were to come up with a generic interface, with a programmable back end to generate the required custom trouble tickets, the AI could save users a lot of time and ensure future efficiencies by ensuring that trouble tickets consistently record the required information.

Understanding how AI reduces boredom

Boredom comes in many packages, and humans view these packages in different ways. There is the boredom that comes from not having required resources, knowledge, or other needs met. Another kind of boredom comes from not knowing what to do next. An AI can help with the first kind of boredom; it can't help with the second. This section considers the first kind of boredom. (The next sec-tion considers the second kind.)

Considering how AI can't reduce boredom

As noted in previous chapters, especially Chapters 4 and 5, an AI is not creative or intuitive. So, asking an AI to think of something for you to do is unlikely to produce satisfying results. Someone could program the AI to track the top ten things you like to do and then select one of them at random, but the result still won't be satisfying because the AI can't take aspects like your current state of mind into account. In fact, even with the best facial expression, an AI will lack the capability to interact with you in a manner that will produce any sort of satisfying result.

An AI also can't motivate you. Think about what happens when a friend comes by to help motivate you (or you motivate the friend). The friend actually relies on a combination of intrapersonal knowledge (empathizing by considering how she'd feel in your situation) and interpersonal knowledge (projecting creative ideas on how to obtain a positive emotional response from you). An AI won't have any of the first kind of knowledge and only extremely limited amounts of the second kind of knowledge, as described in Chapter 1. Consequently, an AI can't reduce your boredom through motivational techniques.

Working in Industrial Settings

Any industrial setting is likely to have safety hazards, no matter how much time, effort, and money is thrown at the problem. You can easily find articles such as: http://www.safetyandhealthmagazine.com/articles/14054-common-workplace-safety-hazards, which describes seven common safety hazards found in industrial settings. Although humans cause many of these problems and boredom makes them worse, the actual environment in which the humans are working causes a great many issues. The following sections describe how automation can help humans live longer and better lives.

Developing various levels of automation

Automation in industrial settings a lot older than you might think. People tend to think of Henry Ford's assembly line as the starting point of automation (see http://www.history.com/this-day-in-history/fords-assembly-line-starts-rolling). In fact, automation began in 1104 AD in Venice (see https:// www.mouser.com/applications/factory-automation-trends/), where 16,000 workers were able to build an entire warship in a single day. Americans repeated that feat with modern ships during WWII (see https://www.nps.gov/nr/ travel/wwiibayarea /shipbuilding .htm). So automation has been around for a long time.

What hasn't been around for a long time is an AI that can actually help humans within the automation process. In many cases today, a human operator begins by outlining how to perform the task, creating a job, and then turns the job over to a computer. An example of one of several new kinds of job is Robot Process Automation (RPA), which allows a human to train software to act in the stead of a human when working with applications (see https:// www.arcusys.com/blog/the-tools-of-the-future-today-what-is-robotic-process-automation-artificial-intelligence-and-machine -learning). This process differs from scripting, such as the use of Visual Basic for Applications (VBA) in Office, in that RPA isn't application specific and doesn't require coding. Many people find it sur-prising that there are actually ten levels of automation, nine of which can rely on an AI. The level you choose is dependent on your application:

- A human operator creates a job and turns it over to a computer to implement.
- An AI helps the human determine job options.
- The AI determines the best job options and then allows the human to accept or reject the recommendation.
- The AI determines the options, uses them to define a series of actions, and then turns the list of actions over to a human for acceptance or rejection of individual actions prior to implementation.
- The AI determines the options, defines a series of actions, creates a job, and then asks for human approval before submitting the job to the computer.
- The AI automatically creates the job and submits it to the computer's job queue, with the human operator acting as an intermediary in case the selected job requires termination prior to actual implementation.
- The AI creates and implements the job and then tells the human operator what it did in case the job requires correction or reversal.
- The AI creates and implements the job, telling the human what it did only when the human asks.
- The AI creates and implements the job without providing any feedback unless a human needs to intervene, such as when an error occurs or the result isn't what was expected.
- The AI initiates the need for the job, rather than waiting for the human to tell it to create the job. The AI provides feedback only when a human must intervene, such as when an error occurs. The AI can provide a level of error correction and manages unexpected results on its own.

Using more than just robots

When thinking about industry, most people think about automation: robots making stuff. However, society is actually in the fourth industrial revolution; we've had steam, mass production, automation, and now communication (see https:// www.engineering.com/ Electronics Design /ElectronicsDesignArticles/ArticleID/8379/New-Chips-are-Bringing-Factory-Automation-into-the-Era-of-Industry-40. aspx for details). An AI requires information from all sorts of sources in order to perform tasks efficiently. It follows that the more informa-tion an industrial setting can obtain from all sorts of sources, the better an AI can perform (assuming that the data is also managed properly). With this in mind, industrial settings of all sorts now rely on an Industrial Communication Engine (ICE) to coordinate communication between all the various sources that an AI requires.

Robots do perform much of the actual work in an industrial setting, but you also need sensors to assess potential risks, such as storms. However, coordination is becoming ever more important to ensuring that operations remain efficient. For example, ensuring that trucks with raw materials arrive at the proper time, while other trucks that haul off finished goods are available when needed, are essential tasks for keeping warehouse floors running efficiently. The AI needs to know about the maintenance status of all equipment to ensure that the equipment receives the best possible care (to improve reliability) and the times when it's least needed (to improve efficiency). The AI would also need to consider issues such as resource cost. Perhaps gaining an advantage is possible by running certain equipment during evening hours when power is less expensive.

Relying on automation alone

Early examples of human-free factories included specialty settings, such as chip factories that required exceptionally clean environments. However, since that early beginning, automation has spread. Because of the dangers to humans and the cost of using humans to perform certain kinds of industrial tasks, you can find many instances today of common factories that require no human intervention at all (see https://singularityhub.com/2010/02/11/no-humans-just-robots-amazing-videos-of-the-modern-factory/for examples).

Creating a Safe Environment

One of the most often stated roles for AI, besides automating tasks, is keeping humans safe in various ways. Articles such as the one at https://futurism. com/7-reasons-you-should-embrace-not-fear-artificial-intelligence/ describe an environment in which AI acts as an intermediary, taking the hit that humans would normally take when a safety issue occurs. Safety takes all sorts of forms. Yes, AI will make working in various environments safer, but it'll also help create a healthier environment and reduce risks associated with common tasks, including surfing the Internet. The following sections offer an overview of the ways in which AI could provide a safer environment.

Considering the role of boredom in accidents

From driving (see http://healthland.time.com/ 2011/01/04/bored-drivers-most-likely-to-have-accidents/) to work (see http://www.universaldrug store.com/news/general-health-news/boredom-increases-accidents-at-workplace/), boredom increases accidents of all sorts. In fact, anytime that someone- is supposed to perform a task that requires any level of focus and instead acts in a somnolent manner, the outcome is seldom good. The problem is so -serious and significant that you can find a wealth of articles on the topic, such as "Modelling human boredom at work: mathematical formulations and a prob-abilistic framework" (http://www.emeraldinsight.com/doi/full/10.1108/ 17410381311327981). Whether an accident actually occurs (or was a close call) depends on random chance. Imagine actually developing algorithms that help determine the probability of accidents happening due to boredom under certain conditions.

Seeing AI in avoiding safety issues

No AI can prevent accidents owing to human causes, such as boredom. In a best-case scenario, when humans decide to actually follow the rules that AI helps cre-ate, the AI can only help avoid potential problems. Unlike with Asimov's robots, there are no three-laws protections in place in any environment; humans must choose to remain safe. With this in mind, an AI could help in these ways:

»» Suggest job rotations (whether in the workplace, in a car, or even at home) to keep tasks interesting

»» Monitor human performance in order to better suggest down time because of fatigue or other factors

 »» Assist humans in performing tasks to combine the intelligence that humans provide with the quick reaction time of the AI

»» Augment human detection capabilities so that potential safety issues become more obvious

»» Take over repetitive tasks so that humans are less likely to become fatigued and participate in the interesting aspects of any job.

Understanding that AI can't eliminate safety issues

Ensuring complete safety implies an ability to see the future. Because the future is unknown, the potential risks to humans at any given time are also unknown because unexpected situations can occur. An unexpected situation is one that the original developers of a particular safety strategy didn't envision. Humans are adept at finding new ways to get into predicaments, partly because we're both curious and creative. Finding a method to overcome the safety provided by an AI is in human nature because humans are inquisitive; we want to see what will -happen if we try something — generally something stupid.

Unpredictable situations aren't the only problem that an AI faces. Even if someone were to find every possible way in which a human could become unsafe, the -processing power required to detect the event and determine a course of action would be astronomical. The AI would work so slowly that its response would always occur too late to make any difference. Consequently, developers of safety equipment that actually requires an AI to perform the required level of safety have to deal in probabilities and then protect against the situations that are most likely to happen.

2.3 Using AI to Address Medical Needs

Medicine is complicated. There is a reason why it can take 15 or more years to train a doctor depending on specialty (see http://work.chron.com/ long-become-doctor-us-7921.html for details). By the time the school system packs a doctor with enough information to nearly burst, most other people have already been in the job force for 11 years (given that most will stop with an associate's or bachelor's degree). Meanwhile, the creation of new technologies, approaches, and so on all conspire to make the task even more complex. At some point, it becomes impossible for any one person to become proficient in even a narrow specialty. Of course, this is a prime reason that an irreplaceable human requires consistent, logical, and unbiased help in the form of an AI. The process begins by helping the doctor monitor patients (as described in the first section this chapter) in ways that humans would simply find impossible because the number of checks is high, the need to perform them in a certain order and in a specific way is critical, and the potential for error is monumental.

Fortunately, people have more options today than ever before for doing many medical-related tasks on their own. For example, the use of games enables a patient to perform some therapy-related tasks alone, yet get guidance from an application that ensures that the person performs the task in a manner most suited to becoming healthy again. Improved prosthetics and other medical aids also enable people to become more independent of professional assistance. The second section of this chapter describes how AI can help assist people with their own medical needs.

Just as it proves difficult, if not impossible, to fix various devices without seeing the device in use in a specific environment, so humans sometimes defy the analysis needed to diagnose problems. Performing analysis in various ways can help a doctor find a specific problem and address it with greater ease. It's entirely possible today for a doctor to fit a patient with a monitoring device, perform remote monitoring, and then rely on an AI to perform an analysis required to diagnose the problem — all without the patient's spending more than one visit at the doctor's office (the one required to attach the monitoring device). In fact, in some cases, such as glucose monitors, the patient may even be able to buy the required device at the store so that the visit to the doctor's office becomes unnecessary as well. Even though the third section of this chapter doesn't provide a view of even a modicum of the various analysis devices, you do get a good overview.

Of course, some interventions require the patient to undergo surgery or other procedures (as described in the fourth section of this chapter). A robotic solution can sometimes perform the task better than the doctor can. In some cases, a robot-assisted solution makes the doctor more efficient and helps focus the doc-tor's attention in areas that only a human can address. The use of various kinds of technology also makes diagnosis easier, faster, and more accurate. For example, using an AI can help a doctor locate the start of cancer far sooner than the doctor could perform the task alone.

Implementing Portable Patient Monitoring

A medical professional isn't always able to tell what is happening with a patient's health simply by listening to their heart, checking vitals, or performing a blood test. The body doesn't always send out useful signals that let a medical professional learn anything at all. In addition, some body functions, such as blood sugar, change over time, so constant monitoring becomes necessary. Going to the doc-tor's office every time you need one of these vitals checked would prove time consuming and possibly not all that useful. Older methods of determining some body characteristics required manual, external intervention on the part of the patient an error-prone process in the best of times. For these reasons, and many more, an AI can help monitor a patient's statistics in a manner that is efficient, less error prone, and more consistent, as described in the following sections.

Wearing helpful monitors

All sorts of monitors fall into the helpful category. In fact, many of these monitors have nothing to do with the medical profession, yet produce positive results for your health. Consider the Moov monitor (https://welcome.moov.cc/), which monitors both heart rate and 3-D movement. The AI for this device tracks these statistics and provides advice on how to create a better workout. You actually get advice on, for example, how your feet are hitting the pavement during running and whether you need to lengthen your stride. The point of devices like these is to ensure that you get the sort of workout that will improve health without risking injury.

Mind you, if a watch-type monitoring device is too large, Motiv (https:// mymotiv.com/) produces a ring that monitors about the same number of things that Moov does, but in a smaller package. This ring even tracks how you sleep to help you get a good night's rest. Rings do tend to come with an assortment of pros and cons. The article at https://www.wareable.com/smart-jewellery/best-smart-rings- 1340 tells you more about these issues. Interestingly enough, many of the pictures on the site don't look anything like a fitness monitor, so you can have fashion and health all in one package.

Of course, if your only goal is to monitor your heart rate, you can get devices such as Apple Watch (https://support.apple.com/en-us/HT204666) that also -provide some level of analysis using an AI. All these devices interact with your smartphone, so you can possibly link the data to still other applications or send it to your doctor as needed.

Relying on critical wearable monitors

A problem with some human conditions is that they change constantly, so checking intermittently doesn't really get the job done. Glucose, the statistic measured by diabetics, is one statistic that falls into this category. The more you monitor the rise and fall of glucose each day, the easier it becomes to change medications and lifestyle to keep diabetes under control. Devices such as the K'Watch (http://www.pkvitality.com/ktrack-glucose/) provide such constant monitoring, along with an app that a person can use to obtain helpful information on managing their diabetes. Of course, people have used intermittent monitoring for years; this device simply provides that extra level of monitoring that can make the difference between having diabetes be a life-altering issue or a minor nuisance.

The act of constantly monitoring someone's blood sugar or other chronic disease statistic might seem like overkill, but it has practical use as well. Products such as Sentrian (http://sentrian.com/) let people use the remote data to predict that a patient will become ill before the event actually occurs. By making changes in patient medications and behaviour before an event can occur, Sentrian reduces the number of unavoidable hospitalizations — making the patient's life a lot better and reducing medical costs.

Completing Analysis in New Ways

Using AI in a manner that most suits its capabilities maximizes the potential for medical specialists to use it in a meaningful way. Data analysis is one area in which AI excels. In fact, entire websites are devoted to the role that AI plays in modern medicine, such as the one at http://medicalfuturist.com/category/blog/digitalized-care/ artificial-intelligence/. Merely taking a picture of a potential tumour site and then viewing the result might seem to be all that a specialist needs to make a great diagnosis. However, most techniques for acquiring the required snapshot rely on going through tissue that isn't part of the tumor site, thereby obscuring the output. In addition, a physician wants to obtain the best information possible when viewing the tumor in its smallest stages.

Not only does using AI to help perform the diagnosis assist in identifying tumors when they're small and with greater accuracy, it also speeds up the analysis process immensely. Time is critical when dealing with many diseases. According to https://www.wired.com/2017/01/look-x-rays-moles-living-ai-coming-job/, the speed increase is monumental and the cost small for using this new approach.

As impressive as the detection and speed capabilities of AI are in this area, what really makes a difference is the capability to combine AI in various ways to perform Internet of Things (IoT) data compilations. When the AI detects a condition in a particular patient, it can automatically check the patient's records and display the relevant information onscreen with the diagnosed scans, as shown in the article at

https://www.itnonline.com/article/how-artificial-intelligence -will-change-medical-imaging. Now the doctor has every last piece of pertinent information for a patient before making a diagnosis and considering a particular path.

Devising New Surgical Techniques

Robots and AI routinely participate in surgical procedures today. In fact, some surgeries would be nearly impossible without the use of robots and AI. However, the history of using this technology isn't very lengthy. The first surgical robot, Arthrobot, made its appearance in 1983 (see http://allaboutroboticsurgery.com/roboticsurgeryhistory.ht ml for details). Even so, the use of these life-saving technologies has reduced errors, improved results, decreased healing time, and generally made surgery less expensive over the long run. The following sec-tions describe the use of robots and AI in various aspects of surgery.

Making surgical suggestions

You can view the whole idea of surgical suggestions in many different ways. For example, an AI could analyze all the data about a patient and provide the surgeon with suggestions about the best approaches to take based on that individual patient's record. The surgeon could perform this task, but it would take longer and might be subject to errors that the AI won't make. The AI doesn't get tired or overlook things; it consistently views all the data available in the same way every time.

Unfortunately, even with an AI assistant, surprises still happen during surgery, which is where the next level of suggestion comes into play. According to the arti-cle at https://www.huffingtonpost.com/entry/the-role-of-ai-in-surgery_ us_58d40b7fe4b002482d6e6f59, doctors can now have access to a device that works along the same lines as Alexa, Siri, and Cortana (the AI in devices you may actually have in your own home). No, the device won't take the doctor's request for music to play during the surgery, but the surgeon can use the device to locate specific bits of information without having to stop. This means that the patient receives the benefit of what amounts to a second opinion to handle unforeseen complications during a surgery. Mind you, the device isn't actually doing anything more than making already existing research created by other doctors readily avail-able in response to surgeon requests; no real thinking is involved.

Getting ready for surgery also means analyzing all those scans that doctors insist on having. Speed is an advantage that AI has over a radiologist. Products such as Enlitic (https://www.enlitic.com/), a deep-learning technology, can analyze radiological scans in milliseconds — up to 10,000 times faster than a radiologist. In addition, the system is 50 percent better at classifying tumors and has a lower false-negative rate (0 percent versus 7 percent) than humans. Another product in this category, Arterys (https://arterys.com/), can perform a cardiac scan in 6 to 10 minutes, rather than the usual hour. Patients don't have to spend time holding their breath, either. Amazingly, this system obtains several dimensions of data: 3-D heart anatomy, blood-flow rate, and blood-flow direction, in this short time. You can see a video about Arterys at https://www.youtube.com/ watch?v=IcooATgPYXc.

Assisting a surgeon

Most robotic help for surgeons today assists, rather than replaces, the surgeon. The first robot surgeon, the PUMA system, appeared in 1986. It performed an extremely delicate neurosurgical biopsy, which is a nonlaparoscopic type of surgery-. Laparoscopic surgery is minimally invasive, with one or more small holes serving to provide access to an organ, such as a gall bladder, for removal or repair. The first robots weren't adept enough to perform this task.

Performing Tasks Using Automation

AI is great at automation. It never deviates from the procedure, never gets tired, and never makes mistakes as long as the initial procedure is correct. Unlike humans, AI never needs a vacation or a break or even an eight-hour day (not that many in the medical profession have that, either). Consequently, the same AI that interacts with a patient for breakfast will do so for lunch and dinner as well. So at the outset, AI has some significant advantages if viewed solely on the bases of consistency, accuracy, and longevity (see the sidebar "Bias, sympathy, and -empathy" for areas in which AI falls short). The following sections discuss various ways in which AI can help with automation through better access to resources, such as data.

Working with medical records

The major way in which an AI helps in medicine is medical records. In the past, everyone used paper records to store patient data. Each patient might also have a blackboard that medical personnel use to record information daily during a hospital stay. Various charts contain patient data, and the doctor might also have notes. Having all these sources of information in so many different places made it hard to keep track of the patient in any significant way. Using an AI, along with a computer database, helps make information accessible, consistent, and reliable. Products such as Google Deepmind Health (https:// deepmind.com/ applied/deepmind-health/ working-partners /health-research- tomorrow/) enable personnel to mine the patient information to see patterns in data that aren't obvious.

Predicting the future

Some truly amazing predictive software based on medical records includes CareSkore (https://www.careskore.com/), which actually uses algorithms to determine the likelihood of a patient's requiring readmission into the hospital after a stay. By performing this task, hospital staff can review reasons for potential readmission and address them before the patient leaves the hospital, making readmission less likely. Along with this strategy, Zephyr Health (https://zephyrhealth.com/) helps doctors evaluate various therapies and choose those most likely to result in a positive outcome — again reducing the risk that a patient will require readmission to the hospital. The video at https://www.youtube. com/watch?v=9y930hioWjw tells you more about Zephyr Health.

In some respects, your genetics form a map of what will happen to you in the future. Consequently, knowing about your genetics can increase your understanding of your strengths and weaknesses, helping you to live a better life. Deep Geno-mics (https://www.deepgenomics.com/) is discovering how mutations in your genetics affect you as a person. Mutations need not always produce a negative result; some mutations actually make people better, so knowing about mutations can be a positive experience, too. Check out the video at https://www.youtube. com/watch?v=hVibPJyf-xg for more details.

Making procedures safer

Doctors need lots of data to make good decisions. However, with data being spread out all over the place, doctors who lack the ability to analyze that disparate data quickly often make imperfect decisions. To make procedures safer, a doctor needs not only access to the data but also some means of organizing and analyzing it in a manner reflecting the doctor's specialty. One such product is Oncora Medical (https://oncoramedical.com/), which collects and organizes medical records for radiation oncologists. As a result, is these doctors can deliver the right amount of radiation to just the right locations to obtain a better result with a lower potential for unanticipated side effects.

Doctors also have trouble obtaining necessary information because the machines they use tend to be expensive and huge. An innovator named Jonathan Rothberg has decided to change all that by using the Butterfly Network (https://www. butterflynetwork.com/#News). Imagine an iPhone-sized device that can per-form both an MRI and an ultrasound. The picture on the website is nothing short of amazing.

Creating better medications

Everyone complains about the price of medications today. Yes, medications can do amazing things for people, but they cost so much that some people end up mort-gaging homes to obtain them. Part of the problem is that testing takes a lot of time. Performing a tissue analysis to observe the effects of a new drug can take up to a year. Fortunately, products such as 3Scan (http://www.3scan.com/) can greatly reduce the time required to obtain the same tissue analysis to as little as one day.

Of course, better still would be the drug company having a better idea of which drugs are likely to work and which aren't before investing any money in research. Atomwise (http://www.atomwise.com/) uses a huge database of molecular structures to perform analyses on which molecules will answer a particular need. In 2015, researchers used Atomwise to create medications that would make Ebola less likely to infect others. The analysis that would have taken human researchers months or possibly years to perform took Atomwise just one day to complete. Imagine this scenario in the midst of a potentially global epidemic. If Atomwise can perform the analysis required to render the virus or bacteria noncontagious in one day, the potential epidemic could be curtailed before becoming widespread.

Drug companies also produce a huge number of drugs. The reason for this impressive productivity, besides profitability, is that every person is just a little different. A drug that performs well and produces no side effects on one person might not perform well at all and could even harm a different person. Turbine (http:// turbine.ai/) enables drug companies to perform drug simulations so that the drug companies can locate the drugs most likely to work with a particular person's body. Turbine's current emphasis is on cancer treatments, but it's easy to see how this same approach could work in many other areas.

Combining Robots and Medical Professionals

Semi-autonomous robots with limited capabilities are starting to become integrated into society. Japan has used these robots for a while now (see https:// www.japantimes.co.jp/news/2017/05/18/national/science-health/japans-nursing-facilities-using-humanoid-robots-improve- lives-safety-elderly/). The robots are also appearing in America in the form of Rudy (seehttp://www.roboticstrends.com/article/rudy_assistive_r obot_helps_ elderly_age_in_place/health_sports). In most cases, these robots can perform- simple tasks, such as reminding people to take medications and playing simple games, without much in the way of intervention. However, when needed, a doctor or other medical professional can take the robot over from a remote location and perform more advanced tasks through the robot. Using this approach means that the person obtains instant help when necessary, reducing potential damage to the patient and keeping costs low.

2.4 Relying on AI to Improve Human Interaction

People interact with each other in myriad ways. In fact, few people realize just how many different ways communication occurs. When many people think about communication, they think about writing or talking. However, interaction can take many other forms, including eye contact, tonal quality, and even scent (see https://www.smithsonianmag.com/science-nature/the-truth-about-pheromones-100363955/). An example of the computer version of enhanced human interaction is the electronic nose, which relies on a combination of electronics, biochemistry, and artificial intelligence to perform its task and has been applied to a wide range of industrial applications and research (see https://www.ncbi.nlm.nih.gov/pmc/articles/PMC3274163/). This chapter concentrates more along the lines of standard communication, however, including body language. You get a better understanding of how AI can enhance human communication through means that are less costly than building your own electronic nose.

AI can also enhance the manner in which people exchange ideas. In some cases, AI provides entirely new methods of communication, but in many cases, AI provides a subtle (or sometimes not so subtle) method of enhancing existing ways to exchange ideas. Humans rely on exchanging ideas to create new technologies, build on existing technologies, or learn about technologies needed to increase an individual's knowledge. Ideas are abstract, which makes exchanging them particularly difficult at times, so AI can provide a needed bridge between people.

At one time, if someone wanted to store their knowledge to share with someone else, they generally relied on writing. In some cases, they could also augment their communication by using graphics of various types. However, only some people can use these two forms of media to gain new knowledge; many people require more, which is why online sources such as YouTube (https://www.youtube. com/) have become so popular. Interestingly enough, you can augment the power of multimedia, which is already substantial, by using AI, and this chapter tells you how.

The final section of this chapter helps you understand how an AI can give you almost superhuman sensory perception. Perhaps you really want that electronic nose after all; it does provide significant advantages in detecting scents that are significantly less aromatic than humans can smell. Imagine being able to smell at the same level that a dog does (which uses 100 million aroma receptors, versus the 1 million aroma receptors that humans possess). It turns out two ways let you achieve this goal: using monitors that a human accesses indirectly, and direct stimulation of human sensory perception.

Developing New Ways to Communicate

Communication involving a developed language initially took place between humans via the spoken versus written word. The only problem with spoken communication is that the two parties must appear near enough together to talk. Consequently, written communication is superior in many respects because it allows time-delayed communications that don't require the two parties to ever see each other. The three main methods of human nonverbal communication rely on:

»» Alphabets: The abstraction of components of human words or symbols

»» Language: The stringing of words or symbols together to create sentences or convey ideas in written form

»» Body language: The augmentation of language with context

The first two methods are direct abstractions of the spoken word. They aren't always easy to implement, but people have been doing so for thousands of years. The body-language component is the hardest to implement because you're trying to create an abstraction of a physical process. Writing helps convey body language using specific terminology, such as that described at https://writerswrite. co.za/cheat-sheets-for-writing-body-language/. However, the written word falls short, so people augment it with symbols, such as emoticons and emoji (read about their differences at https:/ /www.britannica.com /demystified/whats-the-difference-between-emoji-and emoticons). The following sections dis-cuss these issues in more detail.

Creating new alphabets

The introduction to this section discusses two new alphabets used in the computer age: emoticons (http://cool-smileys.com/text-emoticons) and emoji (https://emojipedia.org/). The sites where you find these two graphic alphabets online can list hundreds of them. For the most part, humans can interpret these iconic alphabets without too much trouble because they resemble facial expressions, but an application doesn't have the human sense of art, so computers often require an AI just to figure out what emotion a human is trying to convey with the little pictures. Fortunately, you can find standardized lists, such as the Unicode emoji chart at https://unicode.org/emoji/charts/full-emoji-list. html. Of course, a standardized list doesn't actually help with translation. The article at https://www.geek.com/tech/ai-trained-on-emoji-can-detect-social-media-sarcasm-711313/ provides more details on how someone can train an AI to interpret and react to emoji (and by extension, emoticons). You can actually see an example of this process at work at https://deepmoji.mit.edu/.

The emoticon is an older technology, and many people are trying their best to forget- it (but likely won't succeed). The emoji, however, is new and exciting enough to warrant a movie (see https://www.amazon.com/exec/obidos/ASIN/ B0746ZZR71/datacservip0f-20/). You can also rely on Google's AI to turn your

selfies into emoji (see https://www.fastcodesign.com /90124964/exclusive-new-google-tool-uses-ai-to-create-custom-emoji-of-you-from-a-selfie). Just in case you really don't want to sift through the 2,666 official emoji that Unicode supports (or the 564 quadrillion emoji that Google's Allo, https://allo. google.com/, can generate), you can rely on Dango (https://play.google.com/store/apps /details?id=co.dango.emoji.gif&hl=en) to suggest an appropriate emoji to you (see https://www.technologyreview.com/s/601758/this-app-knows-just-the-right-emoji-for-any-occasion/).

Chapter III

Working with Software-Based AI Applications

3.1 Performing Data Analysis for AI

Amassing data isn't a modern phenomenon; people have amassed data for centuries. No matter whether the information appears in text or numeric form, people have always appreciated how data describes the surrounding

world, and they use it to move civilization forward. Data has a value in itself. By using its content, humanity can learn, transmit critical information to descendants (no need to reinvent the wheel), and effectively act in the world.

People have recently learned that data contains more than surface information. If data is in an appropriate numerical form, you can apply special techniques devised by mathematicians and statisticians, called data analysis techniques, and extract even more knowledge from it. In addition, starting from simple data analysis, you can extract meaningful information and subject data to more advanced analytics using machine learning algorithms capable of predicting the future, classifying information, and effectively making decisions.

Data analysis and machine learning enable people to push data usage beyond previous limits to develop a smarter AI. This chapter introduces you to data analysis. It shows how to use data as a learning tool to solve challenging AI problems such as suggesting the right product to a customer, understanding spoken language, translating English into German, automating car driving, and more.

Defining Data Analysis

The current era is called the Information age not simply because we have become so data rich but also because society has reached a certain maturity in analyzing and extracting information from it. Companies such as Alphabet (Google), Ama-zon, Apple, Facebook, and Microsoft, which have built their businesses on data, are viewed as the top five most valuable companies in the world. Such companies don't simply gather and keep stored data that's provided by their digital pro-cesses; they also know how to make it as valuable as oil by employing precise and elaborate data analysis. Google, for instance, records data from the web in general and from its own search engine, among other things.

You may have encountered the "data is the new oil" mantra in the news, in magazines, or at conferences. The statement implies both that data can make a company rich and that it takes skill and hard work to make this happen. Though many have employed the concept and made it incredibly successful, it was Clive Hum-

bly, a British mathematician, who first equated data to oil, given his experience with consumers' data in the retail sector. Humbly is known for being among the founders of Dunnhumby, a UK marketing company, and the mind behind Tesco's fidelity card program. In 2006, Humbly also emphasized that data is not just money that rains from the sky; it requires effort to make it useful. Just as you can't immediately use unrefined oil because it has to be changed into something else by chemical processes that turn it into gas, plastics, or other chemicals, so data must undergo significant transformations to acquire value.

The most basic data transformations are called data analysis, and you can consider them as the basic chemical transformations that oil undergoes in a refinery before becoming valuable fuel or plastic products. Using just data analysis, you can lay down the foundation for more advanced data analysis processes that you can apply to data. Data analysis, depending on the context, refers to a large body of possible data operations, sometimes specific to certain industries or tasks. You can categorize all these transformations in four large and general families that provide an idea of what happens during data analysis: The interesting interview at https://www.nytimes.com/2014/08/18/technology/ for-big-data-scientists- hurdle-to-insights-is-janitor-work.html with Monica Rogati, who is an expert in the field and an AI advisor to many companies, discusses this issue in more detail.

Understanding why analysis is important

Data analysis is essential to AI. In fact, no modern AI is possible without visualizing, cleaning, transforming, and modeling data before advanced algorithms enter the process and turn it into information of even higher value than before.

In the beginning, when AI consisted of purely algorithmic solutions and expert systems, scientists and experts carefully prepared the data to feed them. There-fore, for instance, if someone wanted an algorithm to sort information, a data expert placed the data into lists (ordered sequences of data elements) or in other data structures that could appropriately contain the information and allow its desired manipulation. At that time, data experts gathered and organized the data so that its content and form were exactly as expected, because it was created for that specific purpose. Manipulating known data into a specific form posed a serious limitation because crafting data required a lot of time and energy; consequently, algorithms received less information than is available today.

Today, the attention has shifted from data production to data preparation by using data analysis. The idea is that various sources already produce data in such large quantities that you can find what you need without having to create special data for the task. For instance, imagine wanting an AI to control your pet door to let cats and dogs in but keep other animals out. Modern AI algorithms learn from task-specific data, which means processing a large number of images showing examples of dogs, cats, and other animals. Most likely, such a huge set of images will arrive from Internet, maybe from social sites or image searches. Previously, accomplishing a similar task meant that algorithms would use just a few specific inputs about shapes, sizes, and distinctive characteristics of the animals, for example. The paucity of data meant that they could accomplish only a few limited tasks. In fact, no examples exist of an AI that can power a pet door using classic algorithms or expert systems.

Data analysis comes to the rescue of modern algorithms by providing information about the images retrieved from the Internet. Using data analysis enables AI to discover the image sizes, variety, number of colors, words used in the image titles, and so on. This is part of inspecting the data and, in this case, that's necessary in order to clean and transform it. For instance, data analysis can help you spot a photo of an animal erroneously labeled a cat (you don't want confuse your AI) and help you transform the images to use the same color format (for example, shades of gray) and the same size.

Specifying the limits of machine learning

Machine learning relies on algorithms to analyze huge datasets. Currently, machine learning can't provide the sort of AI that the movies present. Even the best algorithms can't think, feel, display any form of self-awareness, or exercise free will. What machine learning can do is perform predictive analytics far faster than any human can. As a result, machine learning can help humans work more efficiently. The current state of AI, then, is one of performing analysis, but humans must still consider the implications of that analysis and make the required moral and ethical decisions. Essentially, machine learning provides just the learning part of AI, and that part is nowhere near ready to create an AI of the sort you see in films.

The main point of confusion between learning and intelligence is people's assumption that simply because a machine gets better at its job (learning), it's also aware (intelligence). Nothing supports this view of machine learning. The same phenomenon occurs when people assume that a computer is purposely causing problems for them. The computer can't assign emotions and therefore acts only upon the input provided and the instruction contained within an appli-cation to process that input. A true AI will eventually occur when computers can finally emulate the clever combination used by nature:

»»Genetics: Slow learning from one generation to the next

»»Teaching: Fast learning from organized sources

»» Exploration: Spontaneous learning through media and interactions with others

Apart from the fact that machine learning consists of mathematical functions optimized for a certain purpose, other weaknesses expose the limits of machine learning. You need to consider three important limits:

»» Representation: Representing some problems using mathematical functions isn't easy, especially with complex problems like mimicking a human brain. At the moment, machine learning can solve single, specific problems that answer simple questions, such as "What is this?" and "How much is it?" and "What comes next?"

»» Overfitting: Machine learning algorithms can seem to learn what you care about, but they actually don't. Therefore, their internal functions mostly memorize the data without learning from the data. Overfitting occurs when your algorithm learns too much from your data, up to the point of creating functions and rules that don't exist in reality.

»» Lack of effective generalization because of limited data: The algorithm learns what you teach it. If you provide the algorithm with bad or weird data, it behaves in an unexpected way.

As for representation, a single learner algorithm can learn many different things, but not every algorithm is suited for certain tasks. Some algorithms are general enough that they can play chess, recognize faces on Facebook, and diagnose cancer in patients. An algorithm reduces the data inputs and the expected results of those inputs to a function in every case, but the function is specific to the kind of task you want the algorithm to perform.

The secret to machine learning is generalization. However, with generalization come the problems of overfitting and biased data. The goal is to generalize the output function so that it works on data beyond the training examples. For example, consider a spam filter. Say that your dictionary contains 100,000 words (a small dictionary). A limited training dataset of 4,000 or 5,000 word combinations must create a generalized function that can then find spam in the $2^{100,000}$ combinations that the function will see when working with actual data. In such conditions, the algorithm will seem to learn the rules of the language, but in reality it won't do well. The algorithm may respond correctly to situations similar to those used to train it, but it will be clueless in completely new situations. Or, it can show biases in unexpected ways because of the kind of data used to train it.

For instance, Microsoft trained its AI, Tay, to chat with human beings on Twitter and learn from their answers. Unfortunately, the interactions went haywire because users exposed Tay to hate speech, raising concerns about the goodness of any AI powered by machine learning technology. (You can read some of the story at https://www.theverge.com/2016/3/24/11297050/tay-microsoft-chatbot-racist.) The problem was that the machine learning algorithm was fed bad, unfiltered data (Microsoft didn't use appropriate data analysis to clean and balance the input appropriately), which overfitted the result. The overfitting selected the wrong set of functions to represent the world in a general way as needed to avoid providing nonconformation output, such as hate speech. Other AI trained to chat with humans, such as the award-winning Mitsuku (http://www.mitsuku.com/), aren't exposed to the same risks as Tay because their learning is strictly controlled and supervised by data analysis and human evaluation.

3.2 Employing Machine Learning in AI

Learning has been an important part of AI since the beginning because AI can mimic a human-like level of intelligence. Reaching a level of mimicry that effectively resembles learning took a long time and a variety of approaches.

Today, machine learning can boast a quasi-human level of learning in specific tasks, such as image classification or sound processing, and it's striving to reach a similar level of learning in many other tasks.

Machine learning isn't completely automated. You can't tell a computer to read a book and expect it to understand anything. Automation implies that computers can learn how to program themselves to perform tasks instead of waiting for humans to program them. Currently, automation requires large amounts of human-selected data as well as data analysis and training (again, under human supervision). It's like taking a child by the hand to guide the child's first steps. Moreover, machine learning has other limits, which are dictated by how it learns from data.

Each family of algorithms has specific ways of accomplishing tasks, and this chapter describes those methods. The goal is to understand how AI makes decisions and predictions. Like discovering the man behind the curtain in the Wizard of Oz, you uncover the machinery and the operator behind AI in this chapter.

Taking Many Different Roads to Learning

Just as human beings have different ways to learn from the world, so the scientists who approached the problem of AI learning took different routes. Each one believed in a particular recipe to mimic intelligence. Up to now, no single model has proven superior to any other. The no free lunch theorem of having to pay for each benefit is in full effect. Each of these efforts has proven effective in solving particular problems. Because the algorithms are equivalent in the abstract (see the "No free lunch" sidebar), no one algorithm is superior to the other unless proven in a specific, practical problem. The following sections provide additional information about this concept of using different methods to learn.

Discovering five main approaches to AI learning

An algorithm is a kind of container. It provides a box for storing a method to solve a particular kind of a problem. Algorithms process data through a series of well-defined states. The states need not be deterministic, but the states are defined nonetheless. The goal is to create an output that solves a problem. In some cases, the algorithm receives inputs that help define the output, but the focus is always on the output.

Algorithms must express the transitions between states using a well-defined and formal language that the computer can understand. In processing the data and solving the problem, the algorithm defines, refines, and executes a function. The function is always specific to the kind of problem being addressed by the algorithm.

As described in the "Avoiding AI Hype" section of Chapter 1, each of the five tribes has a different technique and strategy for solving problems that result in unique algorithms. Combining these algorithms should lead eventually to the master algorithm that will be able to solve any given problem. The following sections provide an overview of the five main algorithmic techniques.

Symbolic reasoning

One of the earliest tribes, the symbolists, believed that knowledge could be obtained by operating on symbols (signs that stand for a certain meaning or event) and deriving rules from them. By putting together complex systems of rules, you could attain a logic deduction of the result you wanted to know, thus the symbol-ists shaped their algorithms to produce rules from data. In symbolic reasoning, deduction expands the realm of human knowledge, while induction raises the level of human knowledge. Induction commonly opens new fields of exploration, while deduction explores those fields.

Connections modelled on the brain's neurons

The connectionists are perhaps the most famous of the five tribes. This tribe strives to reproduce the brain's functions by using silicon instead of neurons. Essentially, each of the neurons (created as an algorithm that models the real-world counterpart) solves a small piece of the problem, and using many neurons in parallel solves the problem as a whole.

The use of backpropagation, or backward propagation of errors, seeks to deter-mine the conditions under which errors are removed from networks built to resemble the human neurons by changing the weights (how much a particular input figures into the result) and biases (which features are selected) of the net-work. The goal is to continue changing the weights and biases until such time as the actual output matches the target output. At this point, the artificial neuron fires and passes its solution along to the next neuron in line. The solution created by just one neuron is only part of the whole solution. Each neuron passes information to the next neuron in line until the group of neurons creates a final output. Such a method proved the most effective in human-like tasks such as recognizing objects, understanding written and spoken language, and chatting with humans.

Evolutionary algorithms that test variation

The evolutionaries rely on the principles of evolution to solve problems. In other words, this strategy is based on the survival of the fittest (removing any solutions that don't match the desired output). A fitness function determines the viability of each function in solving a problem. Using a tree structure, the solution method looks for the best solution based on function output. The winner of each level of evolution gets to build the next-level functions. The idea is that the next level will get closer to solving the problem but may not solve it completely, which means that another level is needed. This particular tribe relies heavily on recursion and languages that strongly support recursion to solve problems. An interesting out-put of this strategy has been algorithms that evolve: One generation of algorithms actually builds the next generation.

Bayesian inference

A group of scientists, called Bayesians, perceived that uncertainty was the key aspect to keep an eye on and that learning wasn't assured but rather took place as a continuous updating of previous beliefs that grew more and more accurate. This perception led the Bayesians to adopt statistical methods and, in particular, derivations from Bayes' theorem, which helps you calculate probabilities under specific conditions (for instance, seeing a card of a certain seed, the starting value for a pseudo-random sequence, drawn from a deck after three other cards of same seed).

Systems that learn by analogy

The analogyzers use kernel machines to recognize patterns in data. By recognizing the pattern of one set of inputs and comparing it to the pattern of a known output, you can create a problem solution. The goal is to use similarity to determine the best solution to a problem. It's the kind of reasoning that determines that using a particular solution worked in a given circumstance at some previous time; therefore, using that solution for a similar set of circumstances should also work. One of the most recognizable outputs from this tribe is recommender systems. For example, when you buy a product on Amazon, the recommender system comes up with other, related products that you might also want to buy.

The ultimate goal of machine learning is to combine the technologies and strategies embraced by the five tribes to create a single algorithm (the master algorithm) that can learn anything. Of course, achieving that goal is a long way off. Even so, scientists such as Pedro Domingos (http://homes.cs.washington. edu/~pedrod/) are currently working toward that goal.

Awaiting the next breakthrough

In the 1980s, as expert systems ruled the AI scenery, most scientists and practitio-ners deemed machine learning to be a minor branch of AI that was focused on learning how to best answer simple predictions from the environment (represented by data) using optimization. Today, machine learning has the upper hand in AI, outweighing expert systems in many applications and research developments, and powering AI applications that scientists previously regarded as impossible at such a level of accuracy and performance. Neural networks, the solution proposed by the connectionists, made the breakthrough possible in the last few years by using a mix of increased hardware capacity, more suitable data, and the efforts of scientists such as Geoffrey Hinton, Yann LeCun, Yoshua Bengio, and many others.

The capabilities offered by neural network algorithms (newly branded deep learn-ing because of increased complexity) are increasing daily. Frequent news reports recount the fresh achievements in audio understanding, image and video recogni-tion, language translation, and even lip reading. (Even though deep learning lacks HAL9000 performance, it's approaching human performance; see the article at https://www.theverge.com /2016/11/7/13551210/ai-deep-learning-lip-reading-accuracy   -oxford.)   The improvements are the result of intensive fund-ing from large and small companies to engage researchers and of the availability of powerful software, such as Google's TensorFlow (https://www.tensorflow. org/) and Microsoft's Computational Network Toolkit, CNTK (https://blogs. microsoft.com/ai/2016/01/25/microsoft-releases-cntk-its-open-source-deep-learning-toolkit-on-github),   that   give both scientists and practitioners access to the technology.

Look for even more sensational AI innovations in the near future. Of course, researchers could always hit a wall again, as happened in the previous AI winters. No one can know whether AI will reach the human level using the present tech-nology or someone will discover a master algorithm, as Pedro   Domingos   predicts   (see https://www.youtube.com/watch?v=qIZ5PXLVZfo),   that will solve all AI problems (some of which we have yet to imagine). Nevertheless, machine learning is certainly not a fad driven by hype; it's here to stay, either in its present, improved form, or in the form of new algorithms to come.

3.3 Improving AI with Deep Learning

Newspapers, business magazines, social networks, and nontechnical websites- are all saying the same thing: AI is cool stuff and it's going to revolutionize the world because of deep learning. AI is a far larger field than machine learning, and deep learning is just a small part of machine learning.

It's important to distinguish hype used to lure investors and show what this technology- can actually do, which is the overall purpose of this chapter. The -article at https://blogs.nvidia.com/blog/2016/07/29/whats-difference-artificial-intelligence-machine-learning-deep-learning-ai/ contains a useful comparison of the roles of the three methods of manipulating data (AI, machine learning, and deep learning), which this chapter describes in detail.

This chapter helps you understand deep learning from a practical and technical point of view, and understand what it can achieve in the near term by exploring its possibilities and limitations. The chapter begins with the history and basics of neural networks. It then presents the state-of-the-art results from convolutional neural networks, recurrent neural networks (both for supervised learning), and generative adversarial networks (a kind of unsupervised learning).

Introducing the neuron

Human brains have millions of neurons, which are cells that receive, process, and transmit electric and chemical signals. Each neuron possesses a nucleus with fila-ments that act as inputs, dendrites that receive signals from other neurons, and a single output filament, the axon, that terminates with synapses devoted to outside communication. Neurons connect to other neurons and transmit information between them using chemicals, whereas information inside the neuron itself is electrically processed. You can read more about neuronal structure at http:// www.dummies.com/education/science/biology/whats-the-basic-structure-of-nerves/ or in Neuroscience For Dummies, by Frank Amthor.

Reverse-engineering how a brain processes signals helps the connectionists define neural networks based on biological analogies and their components, using brain terms such as neurons, activation, and connections as names for mathematical operations. Neural networks resemble nothing more than a series of multiplications and summations when you check their math formulations. Yet, these algorithms are extraordinarily effective at solving complex problems such as image and sound recognition, or machine language translation. Using specialized hardware, they can execute prediction computations quickly.

Starting with the miraculous perceptron

The core neural network algorithm is the neuron (also called a unit). Many neurons arranged in an interconnected structure make up a neural network, with each neuron linking to the inputs and outputs of other neurons. Thus, a neuron can input data from examples or transmit the results of other neurons, depending on its location in the neural network.

Frank Rosenblatt at the Cornell Aeronautical Laboratory created the first example of a neuron of this kind, the perceptron, a few decades ago. He devised the perceptron in 1957 under the sponsorship of the United States Naval Research Laboratory (NRL). Rosenblatt was a psychologist as well as a pioneer in the field of artificial intelligence. Proficient in cognitive science, his idea was to create a computer that could learn by trial and error, just as a human does.

The perceptron was just a smart way to trace a separating line in a simple space made by the input data, as shown in Figure 11-1, in which you have two features (in this case, the size and level of domestication of an animal) to use to distinguish two classes (dogs and cats in this example). The perceptron formulation produces a line in a Cartesian space where the examples divide more or less perfectly into groups.- The- approach- is- similar- to- Naive- Bayes,- described- in- Chapter 10,- which- sums conditional probabilities multiplied by general ones in order to classify.

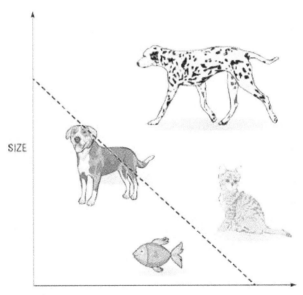

Perceptron-didn't-realize-the-full-expectations-of-its-creato r-or-financial--supporters.- It soon displayed a limited capacity, even in its image-recognition specialization. The-general-disappointment-ignited-the-first-AI-winter-and -abandonment-of-conectionism-until-the-1980s.-Yet,-some -research-continued-despite-the-loss-of-fund-ing- (Dr.- Nils- J. Nilsson,- now- retired- but- formerly- a- Stanford- AI- professor,- tells- more about progress during this time in this article: https://www.singularity weblog.com/ai-is-so-hot-weve-forgotten-all-about-the-ai-winter/).

Later on, experts tried to create a more advanced perceptron, and they succeeded. Neurons in a neural network are a further evolution of the perceptron: They are many, they connect to each other, and they imitate our neurons when they activate under a certain stimulus. In observing human brain functionalities, scientists noticed-that- neurons-receive-signals-but-don't-always-release-a-signal-of-their-o wn.- Releasing a signal depends on the amount of signal received. When a neuron acquires- enough-stimuli,-it-fires-an-answer;-otherwise,-it-remains-silent.-In-a-simi-lar fashion, algorithmic neurons, after receiving data, sum it and use an activation function to evaluate the result. If the input they receive achieves a certain thresh-old, the neuron transforms and transmits the input value; otherwise, it simply dies.

Mimicking the Learning Brain

In a neural network, you must consider the architecture first, which is the arrange-ment of the neural network components. The following sections discuss neural network architectural considerations.

Considering simple neural networks

Contrary to other algorithms, which have a fixed pipeline that determines how algorithms receive and process data, neural networks require that you decide how information flows by fixing the number of units (the neurons) and their distribution in layers called the neural network architecture, as shown in Figure 11-2.

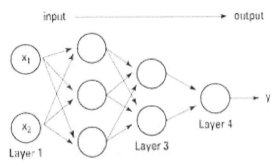

The figure shows a simple neural network architecture. Note how the layers filter and process information in a progressive way. This is a feed-forward input because data feeds one direction into the network. Connections exclusively link units in one layer with units in the following layer (information flows from left to right).

Figuring out the secret is in the weights

Neural networks have different layers, with each one having its own weights. Weights represent the strength of the connection between neurons in the network. When the weight of the connection between two layers is small, it means that the network dumps values flowing between them and signals that taking this route isn't likely to influence the final prediction. Likewise, a large positive or negative value affects the values that the next layer receives, thus determining certain pre-dictions. This approach is analogous to brain cells, which don't stand alone but connect with other cells. As someone grows in experience, connections between neurons tend to weaken or strengthen to activate or deactivate certain brain net-work cell regions, causing other processing or an activity (a reaction to a danger, for instance, if the processed information signals a life-threatening situation).

Each successive layer of neural network units progressively processes values taken from features, as in a conveyor belt. As the network transmits data, it arrives at each unit as a summated value produced by the values present in the previous layer and weighted by connections in the present layer. When the data received from other neurons exceeds a certain threshold, the activation function increases the value stored in the unit; otherwise, it extinguishes the signal by reducing it. After activation function processing, the result is ready to push forward to the next layer's connection. These steps repeat for each layer until the values reach the end, and you have a result.

Understanding the role of backpropagation

Learning occurs in a human brain because of the formation and modification of synapses between neurons, based on stimuli received by trial-and-error experience. Neural networks provide a way to replicate this process as a mathematical formulation called backpropagation. Here's how this architecture of interconnected computing units can solve problems: The units receive an example, and if they don't guess correctly, they retrace the problem in the system of existing weights using backpropagation and fix it by changing some values. This process goes for many iterations before a neural network can learn. Iterations in a neural network are called epochs, a name that fits perfectly because a neural network may need days or weeks of training to learn complex tasks.

Chapter IV

Working with AI in Hardware Applications

4.1 Developing Robots

People often mistake robotics for AI, but robotics are different from AI. Artificial intelligence aims to find solutions to some difficult problems related to human abilities (such as recognizing objects, or understanding speech or text); robotics aims to use machines to perform tasks in the physical world in a partially or completely automated way. It helps to think of AI as the software used to solve problems and of robotics as the hardware for making these solutions a reality.

Robotic hardware may or may not run using AI software. Humans remotely control some robots, as with the da Vinci robot discussed in the "Assisting a surgeon" section of Chapter 7. In many cases, AI does provide augmentation, but the human is still in control. Between these extremes are robots that take abstract orders by humans (such as going from point A to point B on a map or picking up an object) and rely on AI to execute the orders. Other robots autonomously perform assigned tasks without any human intervention. Integrating AI into a robot makes the robot smarter and more useful in performing tasks, but robots don't always need AI to function properly. Human imagination has made the two overlap as a result of sci-fi films and novels.

This chapter explores how this overlap happened and distinguishes between the current realities of robots and how the extensive use of AI solutions could trans-form them. Robots have existed in production since 1960s. This chapter also explores how people are employing robots more and more in industrial work, scientific discovery, medical care, and war. Recent AI discoveries are accelerating this process because they solve difficult problems in robots, such as recognizing objects in the world, predicting human behavior, understanding voice commands, speaking correctly, learning to walk up-straight and, yes, back-flipping, as you can read in this article on recent robotic milestones: https://www.theverge.com/circuitbreaker/2017/11/17 /16671328/boston-dynamics-backflip-robot-atlas.

Defining Robot Roles

Robots are a relatively recent idea. The word comes from the Czech word robota, which means forced labor. The term first appeared in the 1920 play Rossum's Universal Robots, written by Czech author Karel Čapek. However, humanity has long dreamed of mechanical beings. Ancient Greeks developed a myth of a bronze mechanical man, Talus, built by the god of metallurgy, Hephaestus, at the request of Zeus, the father of the gods. The Greek myths also contain references to Hephaestus building other automata, apart from Talus. Automata are self-operated machines that executed specific and predetermined sequences of tasks (as contrasted to robots, which have the flexibility to perform a wide range of tasks). The Greeks actually built water-hydraulic automata that worked the same as an algorithm executed in the physical world. As algorithms, automata -incorporate the intelligence of their creator, thus providing the illusion of being self-aware, reasoning machines.

You find examples of automata in Europe throughout the Greek civilization, the Middle Ages, the Renaissance, and modern times. Many designs by mathematician and inventor Al-Jazari appear in the Middle East (see http://www.fordetails).China and Japan have their own versions of automata. Some automata are complex mechanical designs, but others are complete hoaxes, such as the Mechanical Turk,an eighteenth-century machine that was said to be able to play chess but hid a man inside.

Overcoming the sci-fi view of robots

The first commercialized robot, the Unimate (https://www.robotics.org/joseph-engelberger/unimate. cfm), appeared in 1961. It was simply a robotic arm — a programmable mechanical arm made of metal links and joints — with an end that could grip, spin, or weld manipulated objects according to instructions set by human operators. It was sold to General Motors to use in the production of auto-mobiles. The Unimate had to pick up die-castings from the assembly line and weld them together, a physically dangerous task for human workers. To get an idea of the capabilities of such a machine, check out this video: https://www.youtube.com/ watch?v=hxsWeVtb-JQ. The following sections describe the realities of robots today.

Considering robotic laws

Before the appearance of Unimate, and long before the introduction of many other robot arms employed in industry that started working with human workers in assembling lines, people already knew how robots should look, act, and even think. Isaac Asimov, an American writer renowned for his works in science fiction and popular science, produced a series of novels in the 1950s that suggested a completely different concept of robots from those used in industrial settings.

Defining actual robot capabilities

Not only are existing robot capabilities still far from the human-like robots found in Asimov's works, they're also of different categories. The kind of biped robot imagined by Asimov is currently the rarest and least advanced.

The most frequent category of robots is the robot arm, such as the previously described Unimate. Robots in this category are also called manipulators. You can find them in factories, working as industrial robots, where they assemble and weld at a speed and precision unmatched by human workers. Some manipulators also appear in hospitals to assist in surgical operations. Manipulators have a limited range of motion because they integrate into their location (they might be able to move a little, but not a lot because they lack powerful motors or require an electrical hookup), so they require help from specialized technicians to move to a new location. In addition, manipulators used for production tend to be completely automated (in contrast to surgical devices, which are remote controlled, relying on the surgeon to make medical operation decisions). More than one million manipulators appear throughout the world, half of them located in Japan.

The second largest, and growing, category of robots is that of mobile robots. Their specialty, contrary to manipulators, is to move around by using wheels, rotors, wings, or even legs. In this large category, you can find robots delivering food (https://nypost.com/2017/03/29/dominos-delivery-robots-bring-pizza-to-the-final-frontier/) or books (https://www.digitaltrends.com/cool-tech/amazon-prime-air-delivery-drones-history-progress/) to commercial enterprises, and even exploring Mars (https://mars.nasa.gov/mer/overview/). Mobile robots are mostly unmanned (no one travels with them) and remotely controlled, but autonomy is increasing, and you can expect to see more independent robots in this category.

Working with robots

Different types of robots have different applications. As humans developed and improved the three classes of robots (manipulator, mobile, and humanoid), new fields of application opened to robotics. It's now impossible to enumerate exhaustively all the existing uses for robots, but the following sections touch on some of the most promising and revolutionary uses.

Enhancing economic output

Manipulators, or industrial robots, still account for the largest percentage of operating robots in the world. According to World Robotics 2017, a study compiled by the International Federation of Robotics, by the end of 2016 more than 1,800,000 robots were operating in industry. (Read a summary of the study here: https:// ifr.org/downloads/press/Executive_Summary_WR_2017_I ndustrial_Robots. pdf.) Industrial robots will likely grow to 3,000,000 by 2020 as a result of booming automation in manufacturing. In fact, factories (as an entity) will use robots to become smarter, a concept dubbed Industry 4.0. Thanks to widespread use of the Internet, sensors, data, and robots, Industry 4.0 solutions allow easier customization and higher quality of products in less time than they can achieve without robots. No matter what, robots already operate in dangerous environments, and for tasks such as welding, assembling, painting, and packaging, they operate faster, with higher accuracy, and at lower costs than human workers can.

Taking care of you

Since 1983, robots have assisted surgeons in difficult operations by providing precise and accurate cuts that only robotic arms can provide. Apart from offering remote control of operations (keeping the surgeon out of the operating room to create a more sterile environment), an increase in automated operation is steadily opening the possibility of completed automated surgical operations in the near future, as speculated in this article: https://www.huffingtonpost.com/entry/is-the-future-of-robotic-surgery-already-here_us_58e8d00fe4b0acd784ca589a.

Providing services

Robots provide other care services, both in private and public spaces. The most famous indoor robot is the Roomba vacuum cleaner, a robot that will vacuum the floor of your house by itself (it's a robotic bestseller, having exceeded 3 million units sold), but there are other service robots to consider as well:

»»Deliveries: An example is the Domino's pizza robot (https://www. bloomberg.com/news/articles/2017-03-29/domino-s-will-begin-using-robots-to-deliver-pizzas-in-europe).

»»Lawn mowing: An incredible variety of lawn-mowing robots exist; you can find some in your local garden shop.

»»Information and entertainment: One example is Pepper, which can be found in every SoftBank store in Japan (http://mashable.com/2016/01/27/ softbank-pepper-robot-store/).

»»Elder care: An example of a robot serving the elderly is the Hector, funded by the European Union (https://www.forbes.com/sites/jenniferhicks/ 2012/08/13/hector-robotic-assistance-for-the-elderly/ #5063a3212443).

Assistive robots for elder people are far from offering general assistance the way a real nurse does. Robots focus on critical tasks such as remembering medications, helping patients move from a bed to a wheelchair, checking patient physical conditions, raising an alarm when something is wrong, or simply acting as a companion. For instance, the therapeutic robot Paro provides animal therapy to impaired elders, as you can read in this article at https://www.huffingtonpost.com/ the-conversation-global/robot-revolution-why-tech_b_14559396.html.

Venturing into dangerous environments

Robots go where people can't, or would be at great risk if they did. Some robots have been sent into space (with the NASA Mars rovers Opportunity and Curiosity being the most notable attempts), and more will support future space exploration. (Chapter 16 discusses robots in space.) Many other robots stay on earth and are employed in underground tasks, such as transporting ore in mines or generating maps of tunnels in caves. Underground robots are even exploring sewer systems, as Luigi (a name inspired from the brother of a famous plumber in videogames) does. Luigi is a sewer-trawling robot developed by MIT's Senseable City Lab to

4.2 Flying with Drones

Drones are mobile robots that move in the environment by flying around. Initially connected to warfare, drones have become a powerful innovation for leisure, exploration, commercial delivery, and much more. However, military development still lurks behind developments and causes concern from many AI experts and public figures who foresee them as possibly unstoppable killing machines.

Flying is something that people have done since the Wright brothers first flew on December 17, 1903 (see https://www.nps.gov/wrbr/learn/historyculture/ thefirstflight.htm). However, humans have always wanted to fly, and legend-ary thinkers such as Leonardo da Vinci, a Renaissance genius (more can be discov-ered reading this article from the Smithsonian Museum: https://airandspace. si.edu/stories/editorial/leonardo-da-vinci-and-flight) put their minds to the task. Flying technology is advanced, so drones are more mature than other mobile robots because the key technology to make them work is well understood. The drones' frontier is to incorporate AI. Moving by flying poses some important limits on what drones can achieve, such as the weight they can carry or the actions they can make when arriving at a destination.

This chapter discusses the present state of drones: consumer, commercial, and military. It also explores the roles drones might play in the future. These roles for drones depend partly on integration with AI solutions, which will give them more autonomy and extended capabilities in moving and operating.

Flying unmanned to missions

Resembling a standard airplane (but generally in smaller form), military drones are flying wings; that is, they have wings and one or more propellers (or jet engines) and to some extent aren't very different from airplanes that civilians use for travel. The military versions of drones are now in their sixth generation, as described at https://www.military.com/daily-news/2015/06/17/navy-air-force-to-develop-sixth-generation-unmanned-fighter.html.

Military drones are unmanned and remotely controlled using satellite communications, even from other side of the earth. Military drone operators acquire telemetry information and vision as transmitted from the drone they control, and the operators can use that information to operate the machine by issuing specific commands. Some military drones perform surveillance and recognizance tasks, and thus they sim-ply carry cameras and other devices to acquire information. Others are armed with weapons and can carry out deadly attacks on objectives. Some of the deadliest of these aircraft match the capabilities of manned aircraft (see https://www. military.com/defensetech/2014/11/20/navy-plans-for-fighter-to- replace-the-fa-18-hornet-in-2030s) and can travel anywhere on earth — even to places where a pilot can't easily go (http://spacenews.com/u-s-military-gets-taste-of-new-satellite-technology-for-unmanned-aircraft/).

Military drones have a long history. Just when they began is a topic for much debate, but the Royal Navy began using drone-like planes for target practice in the 1930s (see https://dronewars.net/2014/10/06/rise-of-the-reapers-a-brief-history-of-drones/ for details). The US used actual drones regularly as early as 1945 for targets (see http://www.designation-systems.net/dusrm/m-33.html for details). Starting in 1971, researchers began to apply hobbyist drones to military purposes. John Stuart Foster, Jr., a nuclear physicist who worked for the U.S. -government, had a passion for model airplanes and envisioned the idea of adding weapons to them. That led to the development of two prototypes by the U.S. Defense Advanced Research Projects Agency (DARPA) in 1973, but the use of similar drones in the past decade by Israel in Middle Eastern conflicts was what spurred interest in and further development of military drones. Interestingly enough, 1973 is the year that the military first shot a drone down, using a laser, of all things (see the Popular Science article at https://www.popsci.com/laser-guns-are-targeting-uavs-but-drones-are-fighting-back and Popular Mechanics article at http://www. popularmechanics.com /military/research/a22627/ drone-laser-shot-down-1973/ for details). The first drone killing occurred in 2001 in Afghani-stan (see https://www.theatlantic.com /international/archive/2015/05/america-first-drone-strike-afghanistan/394463/). Of course, a human operator was at the other end of the trigger then.

People debate whether to give military drones AI capabilities. Some feel that doing so would mean that drones could bring destruction and kill people through their own decision-making process. However, AI capabilities could also enable drones to more easily evade destruction or perform other nondestructive tasks, just as AI helps guide cars today. It could even steady a pilot's movements in harsh weather, similar to how the da Vinci system works for surgeons (see the "Assisting a sur-geon" section of Chapter 7 for details). Presently, military drones with killing capabilities are also controversial because the AI would tend to make the act of war abstract and further dehumanizing, reducing it to images transmitted by drones to their operators and to commands issued remotely. Yes, the operator would still make the decision to kill, but the drone would perform the actual act, distancing the operator from the responsibility of the act.

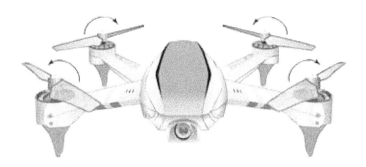

Defining Uses for Drones

Each kind of drone type has current and futuristic applications, and consequently different opportunities to employ AI. The large and small military drones already have their parallel development in terms of technology, and those drones will likely see more use for surveillance, monitoring, and military action in the field. Experts forecast that military uses will likely extend to personal and commercial drones, which generally use different technology from the military ones. (Some overlap exists, such as Duke University's TIKAD, which actually started life in the hobbyist world.)

Apart from rogue uses of small but cheap and easily customizable drones by insurgents and terrorists groups (for an example, see http://www.popularmechanics. com/military/weapons/a18577/isis-packing-drones-with-explosives/), governments are increasingly interested in smaller drones for urban and indoor combat. Indoor places, like corridors or rooms, are where intervention capabilities of aircraft-size Predator and Reaper military drones are limited (unless you need to take down the entire building). The same goes for scout drones, such as Ravens and Pumas, because these drones are made for the operations on the open battle-field, not for indoor warfare. (You can read a detailed analysis of this possible military evolution of otherwise harmless consumer drones in this article from Wired: https://www.wired.com/2017/01/military-may-soon-buy-drones-home/.)

Commercial drones are far from being immediately employed from shop shelves onto the battlefield, although they offer the right platform for the military to develop various technologies using them. An important reason for the military to use commercial drones is that off-the-shelf products are mostly inexpensive compared to standard weaponry, making them both easily disposable and employ-able in swarms comprising large number of them. Easy to hack and modify, they require more protection than their already hardened military counterparts do (their communications and controls could be jammed electronically), and they need the integration of some key software and hardware parts before being effectively deployed in any mission.

Navigating in a closed space requires enhanced abilities to avoid collisions, to get directions without needing a GPS (whose signals aren't easily caught while in a building), and to engage a potential enemy. Moreover, drones would need target-ing abilities for reconnaissance (spotting ambushes and threats) and for taking out targets by themselves. Such advanced characteristics aren't found in present commercial technology, and they would require an AI solution developed specifi-cally for the purpose. Military researchers are actively developing the required additions to gain military advantage. Recent developments in nimble deep learn-ing networks installed on a standard mobile phone, such as YOLO (https:// pjreddie.com/darknet/yolo/) or Google's MobileNets (https://research. googleblog.com/2017/06/mobilenets-open-source-models-for.html), point out how fitting advanced AI into a small drone is achievable given the present technology advances.

Seeing drones in nonmilitary roles

Currently, commercial drones don't have a lot to offer in the way of advanced functionality found in military models. A commercial drone could possibly take a snapshot of you and your surroundings from an aerial perspective. However, even with commercial drones, a few innovative uses will become quite common in the near future:

»»Delivering goods in a timely fashion, no matter the traffic (being developed by Google X, Amazon, and many startups)

»»Performing monitoring for maintenance and project management.

»»Assessing various kinds of damage for insurance

»»Creating field maps and counting herds for farmers

»»Assisting search-and-rescue operations

»»Providing Internet access in remote, unconnected areas (an idea being developed by Facebook)

»»Generating electricity from high-altitude winds

»»Carrying people around from one place to another

Having goods delivered by a drone is something that hit the public's attention early, thanks to promotion by large companies. One of the earliest and most recognized innovators is Amazon (which promises that a service, Amazon Prime Air, will become operative soon: https://www.amazon.com/Amazon-Prime-Air/b?node= 8037720011). Google promises a similar service with its Project Wing (http://www.businessinsider.com/project-wing-update-future-google-drone-delivery-project-2017-6?IR=T). However, we may still be years away from having a feasible and scalable air delivery system based on drones.

Drones can become your eyes, providing vision in situations that are too costly, dan-gerous, or difficult to see by yourself. Remotely controlled or semiautonomous (using AI solutions for image detection or processing sensor data), drones can monitor, maintain, surveil, or search and rescue because they can view any infrastructure from above and accompany and support on-demand human operators in their activities. For instance, drones have successfully inspected power lines, pipelines (https://www.wsj.com/articles/utilities-turn-to-drones-to-inspect-power-lines-and-pipelines-1430881491), and railway infrastructures (http://fortune.com/ 2015/05/29/bnsf-drone-program/), allowing more frequent and less costly monitoring of vital, but not easily accessible, infrastructures. Even insurance companies find them useful for damage assessments (https://www.wsj.com/articles/ insurers-are-set-to-use-drones-to-assess-harveys-property-damage-1504115552).

Police forces and first-responders around the world have found drones useful for a variety of activities, from search-and-rescue operations to forest fire detection and localization, and from border patrol missions to crowd monitoring. Police are finding newer ways to use drones (http://www.foxnews.com/tech/2017/07/19/drones-become-newest-crime-fighting-tool-for-police.html), including finding traffic violators (see the article at http://www.interdrone.com/news/french-police-using-drones-to-catch-traffic-violators).

Agriculture is another important area in which drones are revolutionizing work. Not only can they monitor crops, report progress, and spot problems, but they also apply pesticides or fertilizer only where and when needed, as described by MIT Technology Review (https://www.technologyreview.com/s/526491/ gricultural-drones/).

Powering up drones using AI

With respect to all drone applications, whether consumer, business, or military related, AI is both a game enabler and a game changer. AI allows many applications to become feasible or better executed because of enhanced autonomy and coordination capabilities. Raffaello D'Andrea, a Canadian/Italian/Swiss engineer, professor of dynamic systems and control at ETH Zurich, and drone inventor, demonstrates drone advances in this video: https://www.youtube.com/ watch?v=RCXGpEmFbOw. The video shows how drones can become more autonomous by using AI algorithms. Autonomy affects how a drone flies, reducing the role of humans issuing drone commands by automatically handling obstacle detection and allowing safe navigation in complicated areas. Coordination implies the ability of drones to work together without a central unit to report to and get instructions from, making drones able to exchange information and collaborate in real-time to complete any task.

Taken to its extreme, autonomy may even exclude any human guiding the drone so that the flying machine can determinate the route to take and execute specific tasks by itself. (Humans issue only high-level orders.) When not driven by a pilot, drones rely on GPS to establish an optimal destination path, but that's possible only outdoors, and it's not always precise. Indoor usage increases the need for precision in flight, which requires increased use of other sensor inputs that help the drone understand proximity surrounds (the elements of a building, such as a wall protrusion, that could cause it to crash). The cheapest and lightest of these sensors is the camera that most commercial drones have installed as a default device. But having a camera doesn't suffice because it requires proficiency in pro-cessing images using computer vision and deep learning techniques (discussed in this book, for instance, in Chapter 11 when discussing convolutional networks).

Companies expect autonomous execution of tasks for commercial drones, for instance, making them able to deliver a parcel from the warehouse to the customer and handling any trouble along the way. (As with robots, something always goes wrong that the device must solve using AI on the spot.) Researchers at NASA's Jet Propulsion Laboratory in Pasadena, California have recently tested automated drone flight against a high-skilled professional drone pilot (see https://www. nasa.gov/feature/jpl/drone-race-human-versus-artificial-intelligence for details). Interestingly, the human pilot had the upper hand in this test until he became fatigued, at which point the slower, steadier, and less error-prone drones caught up with him. In the future, you can expect the same as what happened with chess and Go games: Automated drones will outrun humans as drone pilots in terms of both flying skills and endurance.

Understanding regulatory issues

Drones are not the first and only things to fly over clouds, obviously. Decades of commercial and military fights have crowded the skies, requiring both strict reg-ulation and human monitoring control to guarantee safety. In the U.S., the Federal Aviation Administration (FAA) is the organization with the authority to regulate all civil aviation, making decisions about airports and air traffic management. The FAA has issued a series of rules for the UAS (drones), and you can read those regu-lations at https://www.faa.gov/uas/resources/uas_regulations_policy/.

FAA issued a set of rules known as Part 107 in August 2016. These rules outline the use commercial of drones during daylight hours. The complete list of rules appears at https://www.faa.gov/news/fact_sheets/news_story.cfm?new sId=20516. The rules come down to these five straightforward rules:

»»Fly below 400 feet (120 meters) altitude.

»»Fly at speeds less than 100 mph.

»»Keep unmanned aircraft in sight all times.

»»The operator must have an appropriate license.

»»Never fly near manned aircraft, especially near airports.

»»Never fly over groups of people, stadiums, or sporting events.

»»Never fly near emergency response efforts.

The FAA will soon issue rules for drone flight at night that pertain to when it can be out of the line of sight and in urban settings, even though it's currently possible to obtain special waivers from the FAA. The purpose of such regulatory systems is to protect the public safety, given that the impact of drones on our lives still isn't clear. These rules also allow innovation and economic growth to be derived from such a technology.

4.3 Utilizing the AI-Driven Car

A self-driving car (SD car) is an autonomous vehicle, which is a vehicle that can drive by itself from a starting point to a destination without human intervention. Autonomy implies not simply having some tasks automated (such as Active Park Assist demonstrated at https://www.youtube.com/watch?v=xW-MhoLImqg), but being able to perform the right steps to achieve objectives independently. An SD car performs all required tasks on its own, with a human potentially there to observe (and do nothing else). Because SD cars have been part of history for more than 100 years (yes, incredible as that might seem), this chapter begins with a short history of SD cars.

Understanding the Future of Mobility

SD cars aren't a disruptive invention simply because they'll radically change how people perceive cars, but also because their introduction will have a significant impact on society, economics, and urbanization. At present, no SD cars are on the road yet — only prototypes. (You may think that SD cars are already a commercial reality, but the truth is that they're all prototypes. Look, for example, at the article at https://www.wired.com/story/uber-self-driving-cars-pittsburgh/ and you see phrases such as pilot projects used, which you should translate to mean proto-types that aren't ready for prime time.) Many people believe that SD car introduction will require at least another decade, and replacing all the existing car stock with SD cars will take significantly longer. However, even if SD cars are still in the future, you can clearly expect great things from them, as described in the following sections.

Climbing the six levels of autonomy

Foretelling the shape of things to come isn't possible, but many people have at least speculated on the characteristics of self-driving cars. For clarity, SAE International (http://www.sae.org/), an automotive standardization body, published a classification standard for autonomous cars (see the J3016 standard at https://www.smmt. co.uk/wp-content/uploads/sites/2/automated_driving.pdf). Having a standard creates car automation milestones. Here are the five levels of autonomy specified by the SAE standard:

»»Level 1 – driver assistance: Control is still in the hands of the driver, yet the car can perform simple support activities such as controlling the speed. This level of automation includes cruise control, when you set your car to go a certain speed, the stability control, and precharged brakes.

»»Level 2 – partial automation: The car can act more often in lieu of the driver, dealing with acceleration, breaking, and steering if required. The driver's responsibility is to remain alert and maintain control of the car. A partial automation example is the automatic braking that certain car models execute if they spot a possibility collision ahead (a pedestrian crossing the road or another car suddenly stopping). Other examples are adaptive cruise control (which doesn't just control car speed, but also adapts speed to situations such when a car is in front of you), and lane centering. This level has been available on commercial cars since 2013.

»»Level 3 – conditional automation: Most automakers are working on this level as of the writing of this book. Conditional automation means that a car can drive by itself in certain contexts (for instance, only on highways or on unidirectional roads), under speed limits, and under vigilant human control. The automation could prompt the human to resume driving control. One example of this level of automation is recent car models that drive themselves when on a highway and automatically brake when traffic slows because of jams (or gridlock).

»»Level 4 – high automation: The car performs all the driving tasks (steering, throttle, and brake) and monitors any changes in road conditions from departure to destination. This level of automation doesn't require human intervention to operate, but it's accessible only in certain locations and situations, so the driver must be available to take over as required. Vendors expect to introduce this level of automation around 2020.

»»Level 5 – full automation: The car can drive from departure to destination with no human intervention, with a level of ability comparable or superior to a human driver. Level-5 automated cars won't have a steering wheel. This level of automation is expected by 2025.

Even when SD cars achieve level-5 autonomy, you won't see them roaming every road. Such cars are still far in the future, and there could be difficulties ahead. The "Overcoming Uncertainty of Perceptions" section, later in this chapter, discusses some of the obstacles that an AI will encounter when driving a car. The SD car won't happen overnight; it'll probably come about through a progressive -mutation, starting with the gradual introduction of more and more automatic car models. Humans will keep holding the wheel for a long time. What you can expect to see is an AI that assists in both ordinary driving and dangerous conditions to make the driving experience safer. Even when vendors commercialize SD cars, replacing actual stock may take years. The process of revolutionizing road use in urban settings- with SD cars may take 30 years.

Getting into a Self-Driving Car

Creating a SD car, contrary to what people imagine, doesn't consist of putting a robot into the front seat and letting it drive the car. Humans perform myriad tasks to drive a car that a robot wouldn't know how to perform. To create a human-like intelligence requires many systems connecting to each other and working harmoniously together to define a proper and safe driving environment. Some efforts are under way to obtain an end-to-end solution, rather than rely on separate AI solutions for each need. The problem of developing an SD car requires solving many single problems and having the individual solutions work effectively together. For example, recognizing traffic signs and changing lanes require separate systems.

Putting all the tech together

Under the hood of an SD car are systems working together according to the robotic paradigm of sensing, planning, and acting. Everything starts at the sensing level, with many different sensors telling the car different pieces of information:

»»The GPS tells where the car is in the world (with the help of a map system), which translates into latitude, longitude, and altitude coordinates.

»»The radar, ultrasound, and lidar devices spot objects and provide data about their location and movements in terms of changing coordinates in space.

»»The cameras inform the car about its surroundings by providing image snapshots in digital format.

Understanding it is not just AI

After sensing and planning, it's time for the SD car to act. Sensing, planning, and acting are all part of a cycle that repeats until the car reaches its destination and stops after parking. Acting involves the core actions of acceleration, braking, and steering. The instructions are decided during the planning phase, and the car simply executes the actions with controller system aid, such as the Proportional-Integral-Derivative (PID) controller or Model Predictive Control (MPC), which are algorithms that check whether prescribed actions execute correctly and, if not, immediately prescribe suitable countermeasures.

It may sound a bit complicated, but it's just three systems acting, one after the other, from start to end at destination. Each system contains subsystems that solve a single driving problem, as depicted in Figure 14-1, using the fastest and most reliable algorithms.

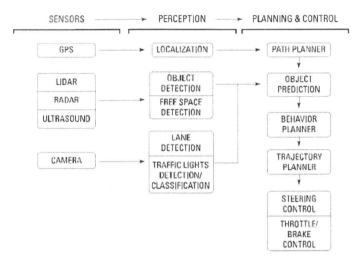

At the time of writing, this framework is the state of the art. SD cars will likely continue as a bundle of software and hardware systems housing different functions- and operations. In some cases, the systems will provide redundant functionality, such as using multiple sensors to track the same external object, or relying on multiple perception processing systems to ensure that you're in the right lane. Redundancy helps ensure zero errors and therefore reduce fatalities. For instance, even when a system like a deep-learning traffic-sign detector fails or is tricked (see https://thehackernews.com/2017/08/self-driving-car-hacking.html), other systems can back it up and minimize or nullify the consequences for the car.

Overcoming Uncertainty of Perceptions

Steven Pinker, professor in the Department of Psychology at Harvard University, says in his book The Language Instinct: How the Mind Creates Language that "in robotics, the easy problems are hard and the hard problems are easy." In fact, an AI playing chess against a master of the game is incredibly successful; however, more mundane activities, such as picking up an object from the table, avoiding a collision with a pedestrian, recognizing a face, or properly answering a question over the phone, can prove quite hard for an AI.

Introducing the car's senses

Sensors are the key components for perceiving the environment, and an SD car can sense in two directions, internal and external:

»»Proprioceptive sensors: Responsible for sensing vehicle state, such as systems status (engine, transmission, braking, and steering), and the vehicle's position in the world by using GPS localization, rotation of the wheels, the speed of the vehicle, and its acceleration

»»Exteroceptive sensors: Responsible for sensing the surrounding environment by using sensors such as camera, lidar, radar, and ultrasonic sensors Both proprioceptive and exteroceptive sensors contribute to SD car autonomy. GPS localization, in particular, provides a guess (possibly viewed as a rough estimate) as to the SD car's location, which is useful at a high level for planning directions and actions aimed at getting the SD car to its destination successfully. The GPS helps an SD car in the way it helps any human driver: providing the right directions.

The exteroceptive sensors (shown in Figure 14-2) help the car specifically in driving. They replace or enhance human senses in a given situation. Each of them offers a different perspective of the environment; each suffers specific limitations; and each excels at different capabilities.

Limitations come in a number of forms. As you explore what sensors do for an SD car, you must consider cost, sensitivity to light, sensitivity to weather, noisy recording (which means that sensitivity of the sensor changes, affecting accu-racy), range, and resolution. On the other hand, capabilities involve the capability to track the velocity, position, height, and distance of objects accurately, as well as the skill to detect what those objects are and how to classify them.

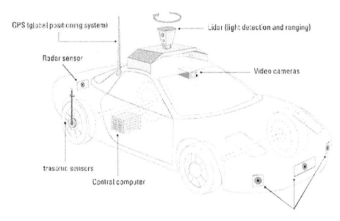

Camera

Cameras are passive, vision-based sensors. They can provide mono or stereo vision. Given their low cost, you can place plenty of them on the front windshield, as well as on front grilles, side mirrors, the rear door, and the rear windshield. Commonly, stereo vision cameras mimic human perception and retrieve information on the road and from nearby vehicles, whereas mono vision cameras are usually special-ized in detecting traffic signs and traffic lights. The data they capture is processed

by algorithms for image processing or by deep-learning neural networks to provide detection and classification information (for instance, spotting a red light or a speed-limit traffic signal). Cameras can have high resolution (they can spot small details) but are sensitive to light and weather conditions (night, fog or snow).

Lidar (LIght Detection And Ranging)

Lidar uses infrared beams (about 900 nanometer wavelength, invisible to human eyes) that can estimate the distance between the sensor and the hit object. They use a rotating swivel to project the beam around and then return estimations in the form of a cloud of collision points, which helps estimate shapes and distances. Depending on price (with higher generally meaning better), lidar can have higher resolution than radar. However, lidar is frailer and easier to get dirty than radar because it's exposed outside the car. (Lidar is the rotating device you see on top of the Google car in this CBS report: https://www.youtube.com/watch?v=_qE5VzuYFPU.)

Radar (RAdio Detection And Ranging)

Based on radio waves that hit a target and bounce back, and whose time of flight defines distance and speed, radar can be located in the front and rear bumper, as well as on the sides of the car. Vendors have used it for years in cars to provide adaptive cruise control, blind-spot warning, collision warning, and avoidance. In contrast to other sensors that need multiple successive measurements, radar can detect an object's speed after a single ping because of the Doppler effect (see http://www.physicsclassroom.com/class/waves/Lesson-3/The-Doppler-Effect). Radar comes in short-range and long-range versions, and can both cre-ate a blueprint of surroundings and be used for localization purposes. Radar is least affected by weather conditions when compared to other types of detection, especially rain or fog, and has 150 degrees of sight and 30–200 meters of range. Its main weakness is the lack of resolution (radar doesn't provide much detail) and inability to detect static objects properly.

Ultrasonic sensors

Ultrasonic sensors are similar to radar but use high-frequency sounds (ultra-sounds, inaudible by humans, but audible by certain animals) instead of micro-waves. The main weakness of ultrasonic sensors (used by manufacturers instead of the frailer and costlier lidars) is their short range.

Putting together what you perceive

When it comes to sensing what is around a SD car, you can rely on a host of differ-ent measurements, depending on the sensors installed on the car. Yet, each sensor has different resolution, range, and noise sensitivity, resulting in different measures for the same situation. In other words, none of them is perfect, and their sensory weaknesses sometimes hinder proper detection. Sonar and radar signals might be absorbed; lidar's rays might pass through transparent solids. In addition, it's possible to fool cameras with reflections or bad light, as described by this article in MIT Technology Review at https://www.technologyreview.com/s/608321/this-image-is-why-self-driving-cars-come-loaded-with-many-types-of-sensors/.

SD cars are here to improve our mobility, which means preserving our lives and those of others. An SD car can't be permitted to fail to detect a pedestrian who suddenly appears in front of it. For safety reasons, vendors focus much effort on sensor fusion, which combines data from different sensors to obtain a unified measurement that's better than any single measurement. Sensor fusion is most commonly the result of using Kalman filter variants (such as the

Extended Kalman Filter or the even more complex Unscented Kalman Filter). Rudolf E. Kálmán was a Hungarian electrical engineer and an inventor who immigrated to the United States during World War II. Because of his invention, which found so many applications in guid-ance, navigation, and vehicle control, from cars to aircraft to spacecraft, Kálmán received the National Medal of Science in 2009 from U.S. President Barack Obama.

A Kalman filter algorithm works by filtering multiple and different measurements taken over time into a single sequence of measurements that provide a real estimate (the previous measurements were inexact manifestations). It operates by first taking all the measurements of a detected object and processing them (the state prediction phase) to estimate the current object position. Then, as new measurements flow in, it uses the new results it obtains and updates the previous ones to obtain a more reliable estimate of the position and velocity of the object (the measurement update phase), as shown in Figure 14-3.

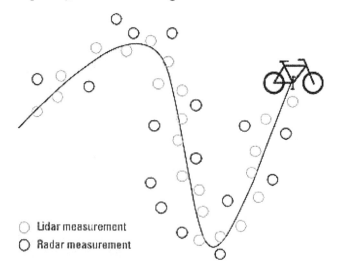

○ Lidar measurement
○ Radar measurement

In this way, an SD car can feed the algorithm the sensor measurements and use them to obtain a resulting estimate of the surrounding objects. The estimate com-bines all the strengths of each sensor and avoids their weaknesses.

Chapter V

Considering the Future of AI

5.1 Understanding the Nonstarter Application

Previous chapters in this book explore what AI is and what it isn't, along with which problems it can solve well and which problems are seemingly out of range. Even with all this information, you can easily recognize a potential application that won't ever see the light of day because AI simply can't address that particular need. This chapter explores the nonstarter application. Perhaps the chapter should be retitled as "Why We Still Need Humans," but the current title is clearer.

As part of this chapter, you discover the effects of attempting to create nonstarter applications. The most worrisome of those effects is the AI winter. An AI winter occurs whenever the promises of AI proponents exceed their capability to deliver, resulting in a loss of funding from entrepreneurs.

AI can also fall into the trap of developing solutions to problems that don't really exist. Yes, the wonders of the solution really do look quite fancy, but unless the solution addresses a real need, no one will buy it. Technologies thrive only when they address needs that users are willing to spend money to obtain. This chapter finishes with a look at solutions to problems that don't exist.

Using AI Where It Won't Work

Table 1-1 in Chapter 1 lists the seven kinds of intelligence. A fully functional soci-ety embraces all seven kinds of intelligence, and different people excel in different kinds of intelligence. When you combine the efforts of all the people, you can address all seven kinds of intelligence in a manner that satisfies society's needs

Defining the limits of AI

When talking to Alexa, you might forget that you're talking with a machine. The machine has no idea of what you're saying, doesn't understand you as a person, and has no real desire to interact with you; it only acts as defined by the algorithms cre-ated for it and the data you provide. Even so, the results are amazing. It's easy to anthropomorphize the AI without realizing it and see it as an extension of a human-like entity. However, an AI lacks the essentials described in the following sections.

Creativity

You can find an endless variety of articles, sites, music, art, writings, and all sorts of supposedly creative output from an AI. The problem with AI is that it can't create anything. When you think about creativity, think about patterns of thought. For example, Beethoven had a distinct way of thinking about music. You can recognize a classic Beethoven piece even if you aren't familiar with all his works because the music has a specific pattern to it, formed by the manner in which Beethoven thought.

An AI can create a new Beethoven piece by viewing his thought process mathematically, which the AI does by learning from Beethoven music examples. The resulting basis for creating a new Beethoven piece is mathematical in nature. In fact, because of the mathematics of patterns, you can hear an AI play Beethoven from the perspective of one of the Beatles at https://techcrunch.com/2016/04/29/paulmccartificial-intelligence/.

Imagination

To create is to define something real, whether it's music, art, writing, or any other activity that results in something that others can see, hear, touch, or interact with in other ways. Imagination is the abstraction of creation, and is therefore even further outside the range of AI capability. Someone can imagine things that aren't real and can never be real. Imagination is the mind wandering across fields of endeavor, playing with what might be if the rules didn't get in the way. True creativity is often the result of a successful imagination.

From a purely human perspective, everyone can imagine something. Imagination sets us apart from everything else and often places us in situations that aren't real at all. The Huffington Post article at https://www.huffingtonpost.com/lamisha-serfwalls/5-reasons-imagination-is-_b_6096368.html provides five reasons that imagination is critical in overcoming the limits of reality.

Just as an AI can't create new patterns of thought or develop new data without using existing sources, it must also exist within the confines of reality. Consequently, it's unlikely that anyone will ever develop an AI with imagination. Not only does imagination require creative intelligence, it also requires intrapersonal intelligence, and an AI possesses neither form of intelligence.

Applying AI incorrectly

The limits of AI define the realm of possibility for applying AI correctly. However, even within this realm, you can obtain an unexpected or unhelpful output. For example, you could provide an AI with various inputs and then ask for a probability of certain events occurring based on those inputs. When sufficient data is available, the AI can produce a result that matches the mathematical basis of the input data. However, the AI can't produce new data, create solutions based on that data, imagine new ways of working with that day, or provide ideas for implementing a solution. All these activities reside within the human realm. All you should expect is a probability prediction.

Entering a world of unrealistic expectations

The previous sections of the chapter discuss how expecting an AI to perform certain tasks or applying it in less than concrete situations will cause problems.

 Unfortunately, humans don't seem to get the idea that the sort of tasks that many of us think an AI can perform will never come about. These unrealistic expectations have many sources, including

»»Media: Books, movies, and other forms of media all seek to obtain an emotional response from us. However, that emotional response is the very source of unrealistic expectations. We imagine that an AI can do something, but it truly can't do those things in the real world.

»»Anthropomorphization: Along with the emotions that media generates, humans also tend to form attachments to everything. People often name their cars, talk to them, and wonder if they're feeling bad when they break down. An AI can't feel, can't understand, can't communicate (really), can't do anything other than crunch numbers — lots and lots of numbers. When the expectation is that the AI will suddenly develop feelings and act human, the result is doomed to failure.

»»Undefined problem: An AI can solve a defined problem, but not an undefined one. You can present a human with a set of potential inputs and expect a human to create a matching question based on extrapolation. Say that a series of tests keeps failing for the most part, but some test subjects do achieve the desired goal. An AI might try to improve test results through interpolation by locating new test subjects with characteristics that match those who survived. However, a human might improve the test results through extrapolation by questioning why some test subjects succeeded and finding the cause, whether the cause is based on test subject characteristics or not (perhaps environmental conditions have changed or the test subject simply has a different attitude). For an AI to solve any problem, however, a human must be able to express that problem in a manner that the AI understands. Undefined problems, those that represent something outside human experience, simply aren't solvable using an AI.

»»Deficient technology: In many places in this book, you find that a problem wasn't solvable at a certain time because of a lack of technology. It isn't realistic to ask an AI to solve a problem when the technology is insufficient. For example, the lack of sensors and processing power would have made creating a self-driving car in the 1960s impossible, yet advances in technology have made such an endeavor possible today.

Considering the Effects of AI Winters

AI winters occur when scientists and others make promises about the benefits of AI that don't come to fruition within an expected time frame, causing funding for AI to dry up and research to continue at only a glacial pace. Since 1956, the world has seen two AI winters. (Right now, the world is in its third AI summer.) The following sections discuss the causes, effects, and results of AI winter in more detail.

Understanding the AI winter

It's hard to say precisely when AI began. After all, even the ancient Greeks dreamed of creating mechanical men, such as those presented in the Greek myths about Hephaestus and Pygmalion's Galatea, and we can assume that these mechanical men would have some sort of intelligence. Consequently, one could argue that the first AI winter actually occurred sometime between the fall of the Roman empire and the time in the middle ages when people dreamed of an alchemical way of placing the mind into matter, such as Jābir ibn Hayyān's Takwin, Paracelsus' homunculus, and Rabbi Judah Loew's Golem. However, these efforts are unfounded stories and not of the scientific sort that would appear later in 1956 with the founding of government-funded artificial intelligence research at Dartmouth College.

Rebuilding expectations with new goals

An AI winter does not necessarily prove devastating. Quite the contrary: Such times can be viewed as an opportunity to stand back and think about the various issues that came up during the rush to develop something amazing. Two major areas of thought benefitted during the first AI winter (along with minor benefits to other areas of thought):

»»Logical programming: This area of thought involves presenting a set of sentences in logical form (executed as an application) that expresses facts and rules about a particular problem domain. Examples of programming languages that use this particular paradigm are Prolog, Answer Set Programming (ASP), and Datalog. This is a form of rule-based programming, which is the underlying technology used for expert systems.

»»Common-sense reasoning: This area of thought uses a method of simulating the human ability to predict the outcome of an event sequence based on the properties, purpose, intentions, and behavior of a particular object. Common-sense reasoning is an essential component in AI because it affects a wide variety of disciplines, including computer vision, robotic manipulation, taxonomic reasoning, action and change, temporal reasoning, and qualitative reasoning.

The second AI winter brought additional changes that have served to bring AI into the focus that it has today. These changes included

»»Using common hardware: At one point, expert systems and other uses of AI relied on specialized hardware. The reason is that common hardware didn't provide the necessary computing power or memory. However, these custom systems proved expensive to maintain, hard to program, and extremely brittle when faced with unusual situations. Common hardware is general purpose in nature and is less prone to issues of having a solution that's attempting to find a problem (see the upcoming "Creating Solutions in Search of a Problem" section of the chapter for details).

»»Seeing a need to learn: Expert systems and other early forms of AI required special programming to meet each need, thereby making them extremely inflexible. It became evident that computers would need to be able to learn from the environment, sensors, and data provided.

»»Creating a flexible environment: The systems that did perform useful work between the first and second AI winters did so in a rigid manner. When the inputs didn't quite match expectations, these systems were apt to produce grotesque errors in the output. It became obvious that any new systems would need to know how to react to real-world data, which is full of errors, incomplete, and often formatted incorrectly.

»»Relying on new strategies: Imagine that you work for the government and have promised all sorts of amazing things based on AI, except that none of them seemed to materialize. That's the problem with the second AI winter: Various governments had tried various ways of making the promises of AI a reality. When the current strategies obviously weren't working, these same governments started looking for other ways to advance computing, some of which have produced interesting results, such as advances in robotics.

Creating Solutions in Search of a Problem

Two people are looking at a mass of wires, wheels, bits of metal, and odd, assorted items that appear to be junk. The first person asks the second, "What does it do?" The second answers, "What doesn't it do?" Yet, the invention that apparently does everything ends up doing nothing at all. The media is rife with examples of the solution looking for a problem. We laugh because everyone has encountered the solution that's in search of a problem before. These solutions end up as so much junk, even when they do work, because they fail to answer a pressing need. The following sections discuss the AI solution in search of a problem in more detail.

Defining a gizmo

When it comes to AI, the world is full of gizmos. Some of those gizmos really are useful, but many aren't, and a few fall between these two extremes. For example, Alexa comes with many useful features, but it also comes with a hoard of gizmos that will leave you scratching your head when you try to use them. This article by John Dvorak may seem overly pessimistic, but it provides food for thought about the sorts of features that Alexa provides: https://www.pcmag.com/commentary/ 354629/just-say-no-to-amazons-echo-show.

An AI gizmo is any application that seems on first glance to do something interesting, but ultimately proves unable to perform useful tasks. Here are some of the common aspects to look for when determining whether something is a gizmo. (The first letter of the each bullet in the list spells the acronym CREEP, meaning, don't create a creepy AI application):

»»Cost effective: Before anyone decides to buy into an AI application, it must prove to cost the same or less than existing solutions. Everyone is looking for a deal. Paying more for a similar benefit will simply not attract attention.

»»Reproducible: The results of an AI application must be reproducible, even when the circumstances of performing the task change. In contrast to procedural solutions to a problem, people expect an AI to adapt — to learn from doing, which means that the bar is set higher on providing reproducible results.

»»Efficient: When an AI solution suddenly consumes huge amounts of resources of any sort, users look elsewhere. Businesses, especially, have become extremely focused on performing tasks with the fewest possible resources.

»»Effective: Simply providing a practical benefit that's cost effective and efficient isn't enough; an AI must also provide a solution that fully addresses a need.

Effective solutions enable someone to allow the automation to perform the task without having to constantly recheck the results or prop the automation up.

»»Practical: A useful application must provide a practical benefit. The benefit must be something that the end user requires, such as access to a road map or reminders to take medication.

Avoiding the infomercial

Bedazzling potential users of your AI application is a sure sign that the application will fail. Oddly enough, the applications that succeed with the greatest ease are those whose purpose and intent are obvious from the outset. A voice recognition application is obvious: You talk, and the computer does something useful in exchange. You don't need to sell anyone on the idea that voice recognition software is useful. This book is filled with a number of these truly useful applications, none of which require the infomercial approach of the hard sell. If people start asking what something does, it's time to rethink the project.

Understanding when humans do it better

This chapter is all about keeping humans in the loop while making use of AI. You've seen sections about things we do better than AI, when an AI can master them at all. Anything that requires imagination, creativity, the discernment of truth, the handling of opinion, or the creation of an idea is best left to humans. Oddly enough, the limits of AI leave a lot of places for humans to go, many of which aren't even possible today because humans are overly engaged in repetitive, boring tasks that an AI could easily do.

Look for a future in which AI acts as an assistant to humans. In fact, you'll see this use of AI more and more as time goes on. The best AI applications will be those that look to assist, rather than replace, humans. Yes, it's true that robots will replace humans in hazardous conditions, but humans will need to make decisions as to how to avoid making those situations worse, which means having a human at a safe location to direct the robot. It's a hand-in-hand collaboration between technology and humans.

Looking for the simple solution

The Keep It Simple, Stupid (KISS) principle is the best idea to keep in mind when it comes to developing AI applications. You can read more about KISS at https://www.techopedia.com/definition/20262/keep-it-simple-stupid-principle-kiss-principle, but the basic idea is to ensure that any solution is the simplest you can make it. All sorts of precedents exist for the use of simple solutions. How-ever, of these, Occam's Razor is probably the most famous (https://science. howstuffworks.com/innovation/scientific-experiments/occams-razor.htm).

Of course, the question arises as to why KISS is so important. The easiest answer is that complexity leads to failure: The more parts something has, the more likely it is to fail. This principle has its roots in mathematics and is easy to prove.

5.2 Seeing AI in Space

People have been observing the heavens since time immemorial. Many of the names of constellations and stars come from the Greeks or other ancients (depending on where you live). The Big Dipper alone has many different names and may be seen as a bear when grouped with other stars (see http:// newsok.com/article/3035192 for details). People love gazing at the stars and thinking about them, which is why many cultures have thought about actually seeing what the stars look like. As people have become capable of space travel, the universe, as a whole, has taken on new meaning, as described in this chapter. AI enables people to see the universe more clearly and view it in new ways.

Over the years, humans have begun living in space (such as at the International Space Station, https://www.nasa.gov/mission_pages/station/main/index. html) and visiting other places, such as the moon. Humans have also begun work-ing in space. Of course, various experiments have produced materials that people can produce only in space. A company, Made In Space (http://madeinspace.us/) actually specializes in this activity. Outside these activities, the use of robots and specialized AI enables the mining of all sorts of materials in space. In fact, the U.S. Congress passed legislation in 2015 making such activity financially feasible (https://www.space.com/31177-space-mining-commercial-spaceflight-congress.html) by giving companies rights to sell what they mine. This chapter also looks at the role of AI in making space-mining work.

The universe holds nearly infinite secrets. One recently discovered secret is the existence of exoplanets, those that exist outside our solar system (see https://www. nasa.gov/feature/jpl/20-intriguing-exoplanets for details).

The existence of exoplanets means that humans might eventually find life on other planets, but even finding the exoplanets requires AI. The ways in which AI will make all these possibilities visible is truly amazing.

Living and working in space is one thing, but vacationing in space is quite another. As early as 2011, people began talking about the possibility of creating a hotel in Near-Earth orbit (http://mashable.com/2011/08/17/commercial-space-station/) or the moon. Although building a hotel in Near-Earth orbit seems feasible- at this point (http://www.newsweek.com/spacex-takes-space-hotel-module-orbit-445616), the moon hotel seems like so much talk (http://www. bbc.com/future/story/20120712-where-is-hiltons-lunar-hotel). The point is, AI will enable people to live, work, and even vacation in space using specialized structures as described in this chapter.

Observing the Universe

A Dutch eyeglass maker named Hans Lippershey is credited with inventing a tele-scope (which at that time, in about 1600, was called Dutch perspective glasses). (Actually, just who invented the telescope is a subject for significant debate; see https://www.space.com/21950-who-invented-the-telescope.html.) Scientists such as the Italian astronomer Galileo Galilei immediately began to scan the skies with something more than their eyes. Thus, telescopes have been around for a long and have become larger, more complex, and even space-based over the years.

Seeing clearly for the first time

One way to avoid earth's atmosphere is to put your telescope in space. However, this approach is a little on the expensive side, and maintenance can become a nightmare. Most people observing the heavens need another alternative, such as a telescope that can adjust for the blurring action of the earth's atmosphere by warping the telescope's mirror (see https://www.space.com/8884-telescope-laser-vision-heavens-blurry.html).

To provide even better optics, future telescopes will feature 3-D correction of blurring effects using multiconjugate adaptive optics (http://eso-ao.indmath. uni-linz.ac.at/index.php/systems/multi-conjugate-adaptive-optics. html). This new technology will correct the narrow field of view suffered by current telescopes, but will require even greater (and more precise) control of multiple actuator levels through multiple mirrors. New telescopes, such as the Giant Magellan Telescope, the Thirty-Meter Telescope, and the European Extremely Large Telescope (see https://www.space.com/8299-world-largest-telescope-built-chile.html) will rely on this technology to make their $1 -billion-plus investment price worth the effort.

Finding new places to go

Before the eighteenth century, people were tied to the surface of the earth, but they still gazed at the heavens and dreamed. Humans tried all sorts of odd experiments, such as tower jumping (see https://jkconnectors.com/news/the--history-of-aviation-part-1/), but before hot air balloons, any sort of true flight seemed out of reach. We still explored, though, and humans continue to explore today, looking for new places to go.

Considering the evolution of the universe

Humans have stared at the universe for a long time and still have no real idea of precisely what the universe is, except to know that we live in it. Of course, the observations continue, but the essence of the universe is still a huge unknown. Recently, scientists have started to use AI to carefully plot the motions of various parts of the universe to try to discover just how the universe works (see https://www.sciencedaily.com/releases/2012/09/120924080307.htm). Using the Lambda Cold Dark Matter (LCDM) model for the cosmos will help humans understand how the universe works a bit better. However, it likely won't even begin to answer all our questions.

Creating new scientific principles

Ultimately, the research that humans perform in learning more about space, the local solar system, the galaxy, and the universe must pay some dividend. Other-wise, no one will want to continue funding it. The AI winters discussed in are an example of what happens to a technology, no matter how promising, when it fails to deliver on expectations. Consequently, given the long his-tory of space exploration, people must be deriving some benefit. In most cases, Performing Space Mining Space mining has received more than a little attention in the media and the scientific-community as well. Movies such as Alien (https://www.amazon.com/xec/obidos/ASIN/B001AQO3QA/ datacservip0f-20/) provide a glimpse as to what a future mining ship might look like. (With luck, space mining won't involve hostile aliens.) Views that are more practical come from articles such as https://www.outerplaces.com/science/item/17125-asteroid-mining-space-erau. In fact, companies such as Deep Space Mining (http://deepspaceindustries.com/ mining/) are already looking into the requirements to perform space mining. What's surprising is that these miners are looking for things like water, which is actually quite common here on earth, but relatively hard to get in space. The following- sections provide further insights into some of the interesting aspects of space mining.

Finding new elements

The periodic table that contains a list of all available elements has received a number of updates over the years. In fact, four new elements appeared in the table in 2016 (see https://www.sciencenews.org/blog/science-ticker/four-newest-elements-periodic-table-get-names).However, finding those four new ele-ments required the work of a minimum of a hundred scientists using advanced AI (see https://www.wired.com/2016/01/smashing-new-elements-into-existence-gets-a-lot-harder-from-here/) because they typically last a fraction of a -second in a lab environment. Interestingly enough, space could provide an environment in which these new elements exist naturally, rather than a fraction of a second because the protons in the nucleus repel each other.

Enhancing communication

Any undertaking in space that is as complex as mining requires the use of advanced communications. Even if the probes and robots used for mining include deep-learning capability to handle most of the minor and some of the major incidents that will occur during the mining process, humans will still need to solve problems that the AI can't. Waiting for hours only to discover that a problem exists, and then spending yet more hours trying to determine the source of the problem, will spell disaster for space-based mining. Current manual communication techniques require an upgrade that, odd as it might seem, also includes AI (seehttps://www.nasa.gov/feature/goddard/2017/nasa-explores-artificial-intelligence-for-space-communications).

Exploring New Places

Space is vast. Humans are unlikely to ever explore it all. Anyone who tells you that all the frontiers are gone has obviously not looked up at the sky. Even the sci-fi authors seem to think that the universe will continue to hold places to explore for humans. Of course, if you like multiverse theory (https://www.space.com/18811-multiple-universes-5-theories.html), the number of places to explore may be infinite. The problem isn't even one of finding somewhere to go; rather, it's one of figuring out which place to go first. The following sections help you understand the role of AI in moving people from planet earth, to other planets, and then to the stars.

Starting with the probe

Humans have already starting putting probes out everywhere to explore every-thing. In fact, using probes is actually older than many people think. As early as 1916, Dr. Robert H. Goddard, an American rocket pioneer, calculated that a rocket could be sent to the moon with an explosive payload that could be seen from earth. However, it was E. Burgess and C. A. Cross who gave the world the term probe as part of a paper they wrote entitled The Martian Probe in 1952. Most people consider a space probe as a vehicle designed to escape earth and explore some other location. The first probe to make a soft landing on the moon was Luna 9 in 1966.

Probes today aren't just trying to reach some location. When they arrive at the location, they perform complex tasks and then radio the results of those tasks back

to scientists on earth. For example, NASA designed the Mars Curiosity probe to determine whether Mars ever hosted microbial life. To perform this task, Curiosity has a complex computer system that can perform many tasks on its own. Waiting for humans simply isn't an option in many cases; some issues require immediate resolution. Curiosity generates so much information that it supports its own blog, podcasts, and website, which you can see at https://www.nasa.gov/mission_ pages/msl/index.html. You can read more about the construction and capabili-ties of Curiosity at https://www.space.com/17963-mars-curiosity.html.

It doesn't take much to imagine the vast amount of information that individual probes, such as Curiosity, generate. Just analyzing the Curiosity data requires the same big data analytics used by organizations such as Netflix and Goldman Sachs (see https://www.forbes.com/sites/bernardmarr/2016/04/14/ama zing-big-data - at - nasa - real - time - analytics - 150 - million - miles - from - earth/#2f5350d35cc4). The different is that the data stream comes from Mars, not from local users, so any data analysis must consider the time required to actu-ally obtain the information. In fact, the time delay between Earth and Mars is as much as 24 minutes. With this in mind, Curiosity and other probes must think for themselves (https://www.popsci.com/artificial-intelligence-curiosity-rover) even when it comes to performing certain kinds of analysis.

After data arrives back on Earth, scientists store and then analyze it. The process, even with the help of AI, will take years. Obviously, reaching the stars will take patience and even more computing power that humans currently possess. With the universe being such a messy place, the use of probes is essential, but the probes may need more autonomy just to find the right places to search.

Relying on robotic missions

Humans aren't likely to ever actually visit a planet directly as a means of learning more about it, sci-fi books and movies notwithstanding. It makes more sense to send robots to planets to discover whether sending humans there is even worth the time, because robots are less expensive and easier to deploy. Humans have actually sent robots to a number of planets and moons in the solar system already, but Mars seems to be a favorite target for a number of reasons:

»»A robotic mission can leave for Mars every 26 months.

»»Mars is in the solar system's habitable zone, so it makes a likely target for colonization.

»»Many scientists believe that life once existed on Mars.

The human love affair with Mars started in October 1960 when the Soviet Union launched Marsnik 1 and Marsnik 2. Unfortunately, neither probe even made it into Earth's orbit, much less to Mars. The U.S. tried next, with the Mariner 3 spacecraft in 1964 and the Mariner 4 spacecraft in 1965. The Mariner 4 fly-by succeeded by sending 12 photos of the red planet back to Earth. Since that time, humans have sent myriad probes to Mars and a host of robots as well, and the robots are start-ing to reveal the secrets of Mars. (The success rate for trips to Mars, however, is less than 50 percent, according to https://www.space.com/16777-curiosity-rover-many-mars-missions.html.) Besides probes designed to perform fly-bys and observe Mars from space, robots land on Mars in two forms:

»»Lander: A robotic device designed to sit in one place and perform relatively complex tasks.

»»Rover: A robotic device that moves from one location to another — increasing the amount of ground covered.

Adding the human element

Humans want to visit other places beyond Earth. Of course, the only place that we've actually visited is the moon. The first such visit occurred on July 20, 1969, with the Apollo 11 mission. Since then, people have landed on the moon six times, ending with the Apollo 17 flight on December 7, 1972. China, India, and Russia all have future plans for moon landings. The Russian-manned flight is scheduled to occur around 2030. NASA plans to land on the moon the future, but no schedule for this event exists yet.

NASA does have plans for Mars. An actual human visit to Mars will likely have to wait until the 2030s (https://www.nasa.gov/content/journey-to-mars-overview). As you might imagine, data science, AI, machine learning, and deep learning will figure prominently in any effort to reach Mars. Because of the distance and the environment, people will require a lot of support to make a Mars landing feasible. In addition, getting back from Mars will be considerably harder than getting back from the moon. Even the lift-off will be harder because of the presence of some atmosphere and greater gravity on Mars.

Building Structures in Space

Just visiting space won't be enough at some point. The reality of space travel is that everything is located so far from everything else that we need waypoints between destinations. Even with waypoints, space travel will require serious effort. However, the waypoints are important even today. Imagine that people actually do start mining the moon. Having a warehouse in Near Earth orbit will be a requirement because of the immense cost of getting mining equipment and other resources moved from the earth's surface. Of course, the reverse trip also has to happen to get the mined resources and finished products from space to earth. People will also want to take vacations in space, and scientists already rely on various structures to continue their investigations. The following sections dis-cuss the use of various structures in different ways to help humanity move from planet Earth to the stars.

Taking your first space vacation

Companies have promised space vacations for some time now. Orbital Technologies made one of the first of these promises in 2011, which had an original expected date of 2016 (see http://www.smh.com.au/technology/sci-tech/space-vacation-orbiting-hotel-ready-for-guests-by-2016-20110818-1j0w6.htmlfor details). The idea was to get there using a Russian Soyuz rocket and to live with six other people for five days. Even though you can't take a space vacation yet, the video at https://www.youtube.com/watch?v=2PEY0VV3ii0 tells you about the technology required to make such a vacation possible. Most of the concepts found in these sites are doable, at least to some extent, but aren't really around today. What you're seeing is vaporware (a promised product that doesn't actually exist yet but is probable enough to attract attention), but it's interesting, anyway.

Performing scientific investigation

A lot of scientific investigation already occurs in space, all of which is currently aided by AI in some way. Everything from the International Space Station to the Hubbard Telescope depends heavily on AI (http://spacenews.com/beyond-- hal-how-artificial-intelligence-is-changing-space-systems/). Regarding the future, you can envision entire labs in space or short-term hops into space to conduct experiments. Zero Gravity currently offers what it terms as a parabolic vomit comet flight to perform near weightless experiments (https://www.gozerog. com/). The flight actually occurs in a plane that goes into a dive from high altitude. This trend is likely to continue, and at higher altitudes.

Industrializing space

Making space travel pay comes in several forms. Humans already enjoy consider-able benefits from technologies developed for space flight and adopted for civilian use here on Earth. (Just one of many articles emphasizing the importance of space to life here on Earth is at https://www.nasa.gov/press-release/spinoff-2016-highlights-space-technologies-used-in-daily-life-on-earth.) However, even with the technology transfers, space is still very expensive, and a better payback could occur by adapting what we know in other ways, such as by creating space factories (https://www.popsci.com/factories-in-space).

In fact, we may find that space factories provide the only way to produce certain materials and products (see https://www.fastcodesign.com/3066988/ mit-invented-the-material-well-need-to-build-in-space as an example). Having a zero-gravity environment affects how materials react and combine, which means that some of what's impossible here on earth suddenly becomes quite possible in space. In addition, some processes are easily performed only in space, such as making a completely round ball bearing (https://www.acorn-ind. co.uk/insight/The-Science-Experiment-Which-Took-Off-Like-A-Rocket---Creating-Space-Ball-Bearings/).

Using space for storage

People will eventually store some items in space, and that makes sense. As space travel becomes more prevalent and humans begin industrializing space; the need to store items such as fuel and mined materials will increase. Because people won't know where mined materials will see use (space factories will require materials, too), keeping the materials in space until a need for them occurs on Earth will actually be less expensive than storing them on Earth. The space gas station might actually appear sooner than you think because we may need it as part of our quest to visit Mars (https://futurism.com/a-gas-station-in-space-could-allow-us-to-reach-other-worlds/ and https://www.smithsonianmag.com/ innovation/nasa-sending-robotic-fueling-station-space-180963663/).

Although no current plans exist for the storage of hazardous materials in space, the future could also see humans storing such waste there, where it can't pollute the planet. Of course, the question of why we'd store hazardous waste, rather than do something like incinerate it in the sun, comes to mind. For that matter, logical minds might question the need to keep producing hazardous waste at all. As long as humans exist, however, we'll continue to produce hazardous waste. Storing such waste in space would give us a chance to find some means of recycling it into something useful, while keeping it out of the way.

5.3 Adding New Human Occupations

When people view news about robots and other automation created by advances in technology, such as AI, they tend to see the negative more than the positive. For example, the article at https://www.theverge.

com/2017/11/30/16719092/automation-robots-jobs-global-800-million-forecast states that using automation will cost between 400 million and 800 million jobs by 2030. It then goes on to tell how these jobs will disappear. Even though the article does admit that some technological advances create jobs (for example, the personal computer created an estimated 18.5 million jobs), the focus is on all those jobs lost and the potential for the loss to become permanent (as they have supposedly become in the industrial sector). The problem is that most of these articles are quite definite when it comes to job losses, but nebulous, at best, when speaking of job creation. The overall goal of this chapter is to clear away the hype, disinformation, and outright fear mongering with some better news.

This chapter looks at interesting new human occupations. But first, don't assume that your job is on the line. (See Chapter 18 for just a few examples of AI-safe occu-pations.) Unless you're involved in something mind-numbingly simple and extremely repetitive, an AI isn't likely to replace you. Quite the contrary, you may find that an AI augments you, enabling you to derive more enjoyment from your occupation. Even so, after reading this chapter, you may just decide to get a little more education and some job training in some truly new and amazing occupation.

Some of the jobs noted in this chapter are a bit on the dangerous side, too. AI will also add a host of mundane applications to the list that you'll perform in an office or perhaps even your home. These are the more interesting entries on the list, and you shouldn't stop looking for that new job if an AI does manage to grab yours. The point is that humans have been in this place multiple times in our history — the most disruptive of which was the industrial revolution — and we've managed to continue to find things to do. If you get nothing else from this chapter, be aware that all the fear mongering in the world is just that: someone trying to make you afraid so that you'll believe something that isn't true.

Living and Working in Space

The media has filled people's heads with this idea that we'll somehow do things like explore the universe or fight major battles in space with aliens who have come to take over the planet. The problem is that most people wouldn't know how to do either of those things. Yet, you can get a job with SpaceX today that involves some sort of space-oriented task (see http://www.spacex.com/careers). The list of potential job opportunities is huge (http://www.spacex.com/careers/list), and many of them are internships so that you can get your feet wet before diving deeply into a career. Of course, you might expect them to be quite technical, but look down the list and you see a bit of everything — including a barista, at the time of this writing. The fact is that space-based careers will include everything that other careers include; you just have the opportunity to eventually work your way up into something more interesting.

Companies like SpaceX are also involved in providing their own educational opportunities and interacting with universities on the outside (http://www. spacex.com/university). Space represents a relatively new venture for humans, so everyone is starting at about the same level, in that everyone is learning some-thing new. One of the most thrilling parts of entering a new area of human endeavor is that we haven't done the things that we're doing now, so there is a learning curve. You could find yourself in a position to make a really big contribution to the human race, but only if you're willing to take on the challenge of dis-covering and taking the risks associated with doing something different.

Today, the opportunities to actually live and work in space are limited, but the opportunities will improve over time. Chapter 16 discusses all sorts of things that humans will do in space eventually, such as mining or performing research. Yes, we'll eventually found cities in space after visiting other planets. Mars could become the next Earth. Many people have described Mars as potentially habitable (see http://www.planetary.org/blogs/guest-logs/2017/20170921-mars-isruech.htmlandhttps://www.nasa.gov/feature/goddard/2017 /mars-mission-sheds-light-on-habitability-of-distant-planets as examples) with thecaveat that we'll have to recreate the Mars magnetosphere (https://phys.org/news/2017-03-nasa-magnetic-shield-mars-atmosphere.html).

Some of the ideas that people are discussing about life in space today don't seem feasible, but they're quite serious about those ideas and, theoretically, they're possible. For example, after the Mars magnetosphere is restored, it should be possible to terraform the planet to make it quite habitable. (Many articles exist on this topic; the one at https://futurism.com/nasa-were-going-to-try-and-make-oxygen-from-the-atmosphere-on-mars/ discusses how we could possibly provide- an oxygen environment.) Some of these changes would happen automatically; others would require intervention from us. Imagine what being part of a terraforming team might be like. To make endeavors like this work, though, humans will rely heavily on AIs, which can actually see things that humans can't and react in ways that humans can't even imagine today. Humans and AIs will work together to reshape places like Mars to meet human needs. More important, these efforts will require huge numbers of people here on Earth, on the moon, in space, and on Mars. Coordination will be essential.

Creating Cities in Hostile Environments

As of this writing, Earth is currently host to 7.6 billion people (http://www. worldometers.info/world-population/), and that number will increase. Today the Earth will add 153,030 people. In 2030, when NASA plans to attempt the first trip to Mars, the Earth will have 8.5 billion people. In short, a lot of people inhabit Earth today, and there will be more of us tomorrow. Eventually, we'll need to find other places to live. If nothing else, we'll need more places to grow food. However, people also want to maintain some of the world's wild places and set aside land for other purposes, too. Fortunately, AI can help us locate suitable places to build, help us discover ways to make the building process work, and help us maintain a suitable environment after a new place is available for use.

As AI and humans become more capable, some of the more hostile places to build become more accessible. Theoretically, we might eventually build habitats in a volcano, but there are certainly a few locations more ideal than that to build before then. The following sections look at just a few of the more interesting places that humans might eventually use as locations for cities. These new locations all provide advantages that humans have never had before — -opportunities for us to expand our knowledge and ability to live in even more hostile places in the future.

Building cities in the ocean

There are multiple ways to build cities in the ocean. However, the two most popu-lar ideas are building floating cities and building cities that sit on the ocean floor. In fact, a floating city is in the planning stages right now off the coast of Tahiti (http://www.dailymail.co.uk/sciencetech/article-4127954/Plans-world-s-floating-city-unveiled.html). The goals for floating cities are many, but here are the more attainable:

»» Protection from rising sea levels

»» Opportunities to try new agricultural methods

»» Growth of new fish-management techniques

» Creation of new kinds of government

People who live on the oceans in floating cities are seasteading (sort of like home-steading, except on the ocean). The initial cities will exist in relatively protected areas. Building on the open ocean is definitely feasible (oil platforms already rely on various kinds of AI to keep them stable and perform other tasks; see https://

www.techemergence.com/artificial-intelligence-in-oil-and-gas/ for details) but expensive.

Underwater cities are also quite feasible, and a number of underwater research labs currently exist (http://www.bbc.com/future/story/20130930-can-we-build-underwater-cities). None of these research labs is in truly deep water, but even at 60 feet deep, they're pretty far down. According to a number of sources, the technology exists to build larger cities, further down, but they'd require better monitoring. That's where AI will likely come into play. The AI could monitor the underwater city from the surface and provide the safety features that such a city would require.

It's important to consider that cities in the ocean might not look anything like cities on land. For example, some architects want to build a underwater city near Tokyo that will look like a giant spiral (http://www.businessinsider.com/ underwater-city-tokyo-japan-2017-1). This spiral could house up to 5,000 people. This particular city would sit at 16,400 feet below the ocean and rely on advanced technologies to provide things like power. It would be a full-fledged city, with labs, restaurants, and schools, for example. No matter how people eventually move to the ocean, the move will require exten-sive use of AI. Some of this AI is already in the development stage (http://news. mit.edu/2017/unlocking-marine-mysteries-artificial-intelligence-1215) as students work with underwater robots. As you can imagine, robots will be part of any underwater city development because they will perform various kinds of maintenance that would be outright impossible for humans to perform.

Creating space-based habitats

A space habitat differs from other forms of space station in that a space habitat is a permanent settlement. The reason to build a space habitat is to provide long-term accommodations for humans. The assumption is that a space habitat will provide a closed-loop environment, one in which people can exist without resupply indefinitely (or nearly so). Consequently, a space habitat would need air and water recycling, a method of growing food, and the means to perform other tasks that short-term space stations don't provide. Although all space stations require an AI to monitor and tune conditions, the AI for a space habitat would be an order of magnitude (or greater) more complex.

Chapter 16 offers some discussion of space-based habitats in the "Taking your first space vacation" section of the chapter. Of course, short visits will be the first way in which people interact with space. A space vacation would certainly be interesting! However, a Near Earth vacation is different from a long-term habitat in deep space, which NASA will need if it actually succeeds in making a trip to Mars a reality. NASA has already commissioned six companies to start looking into the requirements for creating habitats in deep space (https://www.nasa. gov/press-release/nasa-selects-six-companies-to-develop-prototypes-concepts-for-deep-space-habitats). You can see some of the prototypes that these companies created at https://www.nasa.gov/feature/nextstep-partnerships-develop-ground-prototypes.

or some organizations, space-based habitats aren't so much a means for enhancing exploration but rather for protecting civilization. At this moment, if a giant asteroid impacts Earth, most of humanity will perish. People on the

International Space Station (ISS) might survive, however — at least, if the asteroid didn't hit it as well. However, the ISS isn't a long-term survival strategy for humans, and the number of people on the ISS at any given time is limited. So, people like the Life-boat Foundation (https://lifeboat.com/ex/spacehabitats) are looking into space habitats as a means for ensuring humanity's survival. Their first attempt at a space habitat is Ark I (https://lifeboat.com/ex/arki), which is designed for 1,000 permanent residents and up to 500 guests. Theoretically, the technology can work, but it will require a great deal of planning.

Another use for space habitats is as a generational ship, a kind of vessel to explore interstellar space using technologies we have available today. People would live on this ship as it traveled to the stars. They'd have children in space in order to make long voyages feasible. The idea of generational ships isn't new. They have appeared in both movies and books for years. However, you can read about the efforts to create a real generational ship at http://www.icarusinterstellar.org/building-blocks-for-a-generation-ship. The problem with a generational ship is that the ship would require a consistent number of people who are willing to work in each of the various trades needed to keep the ship moving. Even so, growing up knowing that you have an essential job waiting for you would be an interesting change from what humans have to deal with today.

Rather than build space habitat components on Earth and then moving them into space, the current strategy is to mine the materials needed from asteroids and use space factories to produce the space habitats. The solar system's main asteroid belt is currently estimated to contain enough material to build habitats containing the same area as 3,000 Earths. That's a lot of human beings in space.

Constructing moon-based resources

It's not a matter of if we go back to the moon and build bases there; it's when. Many of the current strategies for colonizing space depend on moon-based resources of various sorts, including the NASA effort to eventually send people to Mars. We don't suffer from any lack of moon base designs, either. You can see a few of these designs at https://interestingengineering.com/8-interesting-moon-base-proposals-every-space-enthusiast-should-see.

At times, people have talked of military bases on the moon (http://www.todayi foundout.com/index.php /2017/01 /project -horizon/), but the Outer Space Treaty, signed by 60 nations as a way to keep politics out of space (http://www.unoosa.org/oosa/en/ourwork/spacelaw/treaties/ introouterspacetreaty.html) has largely put an end to that idea. Moon-based structures and the services they provide will more likely answer exploration, mining, and factory needs at first, followed by complete cities. Even though these projects will likely rely on robots, they will still require humans to perform a wide range of tasks, including robot repair and robot management. Building bases on the moon will also require a host of new occupations that you won't likely see as part of habitats or in scenarios that deal exclusively with working in space. For example, someone will have to deal with the aftermath of moonquakes (see https://science.nasa.gov/science-news/science-at-nasa/2006/15mar_moonquakesfor details).

Significant use of AI will occur no matter how we decided to live and work in space. The way we create the AI will differ depending on where we go and when. People currently have the idea that we could be living on Mars in a relatively short period. However, when reviewing sites such as https://phys.org/news/2017-03-future-space-colonization-terraforming-habitats.html, it becomes obvious that terraforming Mars will take a very long time indeed. Just to warm the planet (after we build the technology required to recreate the Mars magnetosphere) will take about a hundred years. Consequently, we don't really have a choice between habitats and terraforming; habitats will come first, and we'll likely use them extensively to make any plans we have for Mars work. Even so, the AI for both projects will be different, and seeing the sorts of problems that the AI will help address should be interesting.

Using existing moon features to build housing is also a possibility. The recent discovery of moon structures suitable to colonization uses would make building bases on the moon easier. For example, you can read about a huge cave that's suitable for colonization at http://time.com/4990676/moon-cave-base-lunar-colony-exploration/. In this case, Japan discovered what appears to be a lava tube that would protect colonists from a variety of environmental threats.

Of course, the hype surrounding some of these structures (very likely natural in origin) is nothing short of amazing. Some sources claim that structures on the far side of the moon are built by aliens (http://www.dailymail.co.uk /sciencetech/ article-4308270/UFO-hunters-claim-footage-aliens-moon.html). The pic-tures at https://www.youtube.com /watch?v=3caLr89zccw are clearer. Remem-ber: Everything is open to hype. The structures exist; we can use them to help make base building easier; and you should probably keep your options open with regard to believing these information sources.

Making Humans More Efficient

An AI can make a human more efficient in lots of different ways. Most of the chapters in this book have some sort of example of a human relying on an AI to do things more efficiently. One of the more interesting chapters, though, is Chapter- 7, which points out how an AI will help with medical needs in various ways. All these uses of an AI assume that a human remains in charge but uses the AI to become better at performing a task. For example, the da Vinci Surgical System doesn't replace the surgeon; it simply makes the surgeon able to perform the task with greater ease and less potential for errors. A new occupation that goes along with this effort is a trainer who shows professionals how to use new tools that include an AI.

In the future, you should plan to see consultants whose only job is to find new ways to incorporate AIs into business processes to help people become more efficient. To some extent, this profession already exists, but the need will increase at some point when generic, configurable AIs become common. For many businesses, the key to profitability will hinge on finding the right AI to augment human workers so that workers can complete tasks without error and as quickly as possible. Think about these people as part script programmer/application packager, part salesperson, and part trainer all wrapped into one. You can see an example of this kind of thinking in the article at http://www.information-age.com/ harness-ai-improve-workplace-efficiency-123469118/.

When dealing with human efficiency, you should think about areas in which an AI can excel. For example, an AI wouldn't work well in a creative task, so you leave the creativity to a human. However, an AI does perform searches exceptionally well, so you might train a human to rely on an AI to perform search-related tasks while the human does something creative. Here are some ways in which you may see humans using an AI to become more efficient in the future:

»» Hiring: Currently, a person hiring people for an organization may not know all the candidate's real credentials and history. An AI could research candidates before an interview so that the hiring person has more information to use during the interview. In addition, because the AI would use the same search methodology for every candidate, the organization can ensure that each candidate is treated both fairly and equally. The article at https://www. forbes.com/sites/georgenehuang/2017/09/27/why-ai-doesnt-mean-taking-the-human-out-of-human-resources/#41767af81ea6 provides additional details on this particular task. The consumer goods company, Unilever, is also using such technology, as described at http://www. businessinsider.com/unilever-artificial-intelligence-hiring-process-2017-6.

»» Scheduling: Today, a business is constantly at risk because someone didn't think about the need to schedule a task. In fact, people might not have had time to even think about the need for the task in the first place. Secretaries and assistants used to manage schedules, but in the new, flattened, hierarchies, these assistants have disappeared, and individual employees perform their own scheduling tasks. Thus, overworked employees often miss opportunities to help a business excel because they're too busy managing a schedule. Coupling an AI with a human frees the human from actually performing the scheduling. Instead, the human can look ahead and see what will need to be scheduled. It's a matter of focus: By focusing the human where the human can excel, the business gets more out of the human. The AI makes this focus on human excellence possible.

»» Locating hidden information: More than ever today, businesses get blindsided by the competition because of hidden information. Information overload and ever growing science, technology, business, and society complexity are at the root of the problem. Perhaps a new way to package goods exists that reduces costs significantly, or the structure of a business changes as a result of internal politics. Knowing what is available and what's going on at all times is the only way that businesses can truly succeed, but the job is simply not feasible. If a human were to take the time required to become all-knowing about everything that a particular job requires, no time would be left to actually do the job.

AIs, however, are exceptional at finding things. By incorporating machine learning into the mix, a human could train an AI to look for precisely the right issues and requirements to keep a business afloat without wasting quite so much time in manual searches.

»» Adaptive help: Anyone using products today will have to admit that having to remember how to perform a certain task is incredibly frustrating at times, especially when rediscovering how to perform the task requires using application help. You can already see how an AI becomes an adaptive aid when it comes to typing certain kinds of information into forms. However, an AI could go much further. By using machine learning techniques to discover patterns of use, an AI could eventually provide adaptive help that would help users get past hard-to-remember parts of an application. Because every user is different, an application that is hardwired to provide adaptive help would never work. Using machine learning enables people to customize the help system to fit each individual user.

»» Adaptive learning: Today you can take an adaptive exam that tailors itself to ask questions about perceived weak areas in your knowledge. The adaptive exam either discovers that you really do know enough or asks enough questions to ensure that you need more training. Eventually, applications will be able to sense how you use them and then provide automated training to make you better. For example, the application may discover that you could perform a task using five fewer clicks, so it could show you how to perform the task using this approach. By constantly training people to use the most efficient approach when interacting with computers or performing other tasks, the person becomes more efficient but the need for the human in that particular role remains.

Fixing Problems on a Planetary Scale

Regardless of whether you believe in global warming, think that pollution is a problem, or are concerned about overpopulation, the fact is that we have only one planet Earth, and it has problems. The weather is most definitely getting stranger; large areas are no longer useful because of pollution; and some areas of the world have, frankly, too many people. An out-of-control storm or forest fire doesn't care what you think; the result is always the same: destruction of areas where humans live. The act of trying to cram too many people into too little space usually results in disease, crime, and other problems. The issues aren't political or defined by personal beliefs. The issues are real, and AI can help solve them by helping knowledgeable people look for the right patterns. The following sections discuss planetary problems from the perspective of using an AI to see, understand, and potentially fix them. We're not stating or implying any political or other kind of message.

Contemplating how the world works

Sensors monitor every aspect of the planet today. In fact, so much information exists that it's amazing that anyone can collect all of it in one place, much less do anything with it. In addition, because of the interactions among various Earth environments, you can't really know which facts have a causal effect on some other part of the environment. For example, it's hard to know precisely how much wind patterns affect sea warming, which in turn affects currents that potentially produce storms. If humans actually understood all these various interactions, the weather report would be more accurate. Unfortunately, the weather report is usu-ally sort of right — if you squint just right and hold your mouth a certain way. The fact that we accept this level of performance from the people who predict the weather testifies to our awareness of the difficulty of the task.

Over the years, weather prediction has become a lot more reliable. Part of the rea-son for this increase in reliability is all those sensors out there. The weather service has also created better weather models and amassed a much larger store of data to use for predictions. However, the overriding reason that the weather report is more accurate is the use of AI to handle the number crunching and look for identifiable patterns in the resulting data (see https://www.techemergence.com/ai-for-weather-forecasting/ for details).

The weather is actually one of the better understood Earth processes. Consider the difficulty in forecasting earthquakes. The use of machine learning has made it

more likely that scientists will know when an earthquake will happen (https:// www.express.co.uk/news/science /871022/earthquake-artificial-intelligence-AI-cambridge-university), but only time will tell whether the new information is actually useful. At one time people thought that the weather could affect earthquakes, but this isn't the case. On the other hand, earthquakes can affect the weather by changing the environmental conditions. Also, earth-quakes and weather can combine to make a situation even worse (https://www. usatoday.com/story/news/nation/2015/05/02/kostigen-earthquake-weather/26649071/).

Even more difficult to predict are volcanic eruptions. At least NASA can now detect and obtain images of volcanic eruptions with great accuracy (https://www. livescience.com/58423-nasa-artificial-intelligence-captures-volcano- eruption.html). Volcanic eruptions often cause earthquakes, so knowing about one helps to predict the other (http://volcano.oregonstate.edu/how-are-volcanoes-and-earthquakes-related). Of course, volcanoes also affect the weather (http://volcano.oregonstate.edu/how-do-volcanoes-affect-atmosphere-and-climate).

The natural events that this section has covered so far are just the tip of the ice-berg. If you're getting the idea that Earth is so complex that no one person could ever understand it, you're right. That's why we need to create and train AIs to help humans do a better job of understanding how the world works. By creating this sort of knowledge, avoiding catastrophic events in the future may be possible, along with reducing the effects of certain manmade ills.

No matter what you've read, no way currently exists to prevent bad weather, earthquakes, or volcanos. The best that humans can hope to achieve today is to predict these events and then act to reduce their impact. However, even the ability to reduce the impact of natural events is a major step forward. Before AI, humans were at the mercy of whatever event occurred because prediction was impossible before it was too late to truly act in a proactive manner to reduce the effects of the natural disaster.

Likewise, even though preventing all manmade disasters might seem possible, it often isn't. No amount of planning will keep accidents from happening. This said, most human-made events are controllable and potentially preventable with the correct insights, which can be provided through the pattern matching that an AI can provide.

Locating potential sources of problems

With all the eyes in the sky today, you'd think that satellite data could provide an absolute source of data for predicting problems on earth. However, this viewpoint has a number of problems:

»» The Earth is huge, so detecting a particular event means scouring millions of pictures every second of every day.

»» The pictures must appear at the correct resolution to actually find an event.

»» Using the right light filter is essential because some events become visible only in the right light.

»» Weather can prevent the acquisition of certain types of images.

Even with all these problems, scientists and others use AI to scan through the pictures taken each day, looking for potential problems (https://www.cnet.com/ news/descartes-labs-satellite-imagery-artificial-intelligence-- geovisual-search/). However, the AI can show possible problem areas and -perform analysis only when the images appear in the correct form. A human still has to determine whether the problem is real and needs to be addressed. For example, a major storm in the middle of the Pacific Ocean away from the trans-portation routes or any landmass probably won't be considered a high-priority problem. The same storm over the top of a landmass is a cause for concern. Of course, when it comes to storms, detecting the storm before it becomes an issue is always better than trying to do something about it later.

Besides scanning images for potential problems, AI can also enhance images. The article at https://www.wired.com/story/how-ai-could-really-enhance-images-from-space/ talks about how AI can increase the resolution and usability of images taken from space. By enhancing the images, the AI can make better determinations of specific kinds of events based on the event pattern. Of course, if the AI hasn't seen a particular pattern before, it still can't make any sort of pre-diction. Humans will always need to check the AI and ensure that an event really is what the AI purports it to be.

Defining potential solutions

The solution to planetary problems depends on the problem. For example, with a storm, earthquake, or volcanic eruption, preventing the event isn't even a consideration. The best that humans can hope to achieve today is to get the area of the event evacuated and provide people with another place to go. However, by knowing as much about the event as possible as far in advance as possible, people can act proactively rather than react to the event after total chaos breaks out.

Other events don't necessarily require an evacuation. For example, with current technology and a bit of luck, people can reduce the effects of something like a forest fire. In fact, some fire professionals are now using AI to actually predict forest fires before they occur (https://www.ctvnews.ca/sci-tech/artificial-intelligence-can-better-predict-forest-fires-says-alberta-researcher-1.3542249). Using AI to enable people to see the problem and then create a solution for it based on historical data is feasible because humans have recorded so much information about these events in the past.

Using historical data to work through planetary problems is essential. Having just one potential solution is usually a bad idea. The best plans for solving a problem include several solutions, and an AI can help rank the potential solutions based on historical results. Of course, here again, a human may see something in the solutions that makes one option preferable to another. For example, a particularsolution may not work because the resources aren't available or the people involved don't have the right training.

Seeing the effects of the solutions

Tracking the results of a particular solution means recording data in real time, analyzing it as quickly as possible, and then displaying the effects in a way that humans understand. An AI can gather data, analyze it, and provide several pre-sentations of that data far faster than any human can do it.

Humans are still set-ting the criteria for performing all these tasks and making the final decisions; the AI simply acts as a tool to enable the human to act in a reasonable amount of time.

In the future, some people might specialize in interacting with AIs to make them work with data better. Getting the right results often means knowing what question to ask and how to ask it. People today often get poor results from an AI because they aren't familiar enough with how the AI works to ask reasonable questions of it.

Humans who assume that AIs think in a human-like manner are doomed to fail at getting good results from the AI. Of course, that's what our society promotes today. The Siri and Alexa commercials make the AI appear to be human, but it isn't, of course. In an emergency, even with an AI accessible to the humans who are dealing with the event, the humans must know how to ask appropriate questions and in what way to ask them to get the required results. You can't see the effect of a solution if you don't know what to expect from the AI.

Trying again

The Earth is a complicated place. Various factors interact with other factors in ways that no one can anticipate. Consequently, the solution you created may not actually solve a problem. In fact, if you read the news very often, you find that many solutions don't solve anything at all. Trial and error help people understand what does and doesn't work. However, by using an AI to recognize patterns of failure — those solutions that didn't work, and why — you can reduce the number of solutions that you need to try to find one that works. In addition, an AI can look for similar scenarios for solutions that have worked in the past, sometimes saving time and effort in trying to find new solutions to try. AI isn't a magic wand that you can wave to create a solution that works the first time you try it. The reason that humans will always remain in the picture is that only humans can see the results for what they are.

An AI is always programmed to win today. The "Understanding teaching orienta-tion" sidebar in Chapter 13 discusses the potential for creating an AI that under-stands futility — that is, the no-win scenario. However, such an AI doesn't currently exist and may never exist. Humans, however, do understand the no-win scenario and can therefore often create a less-than-optimal solution that works well enough. In assessing why a solution doesn't work, considering the no-win scenario is essential because the AI will never present it to you.

The AIs you use in creating solutions will eventually run out of ideas, at which point the AI becomes basically useless. That's because an AI isn't creative. The patterns that an AI works with already exist. However, those patterns may not address a current need, which means that you need new patterns. Humans are adept at creating new patterns to apply to problems. Consequently, trying again becomes essential as a means to create new patterns that an AI can then access and use to help a human remember something that worked in the past. In short, humans are an essential part of the problem-solving loop.

www.ingramcontent.com/pod-product-compliance
Lightning Source LLC
Chambersburg PA
CBHW070948050326
40689CB00014B/3384